DEAR BOSS

DEAR BOSS

What Every Manager
Needs to Hear
and
Every Employee
Wants to Say

William B. Werther, Jr., Ph.D.

Meadowbrook Press
Distributed by Simon & Schuster
New York

Library of Congress Cataloging-in-Publication Data
Werther, William B.
    Dear boss.
    1. Personnel management. 2. Supervisors. 3. Supervision of
employees.   I. Title.
HF5549.W4385   1989   658.3   88-37752
ISBN: 0-88166-166-X

Editor: Katherine Stevenson
Production Editor: Cassandra McCullough
Art Director: Maria Mazzara
Production Manager: Pam Scheunemann

Simon & Schuster Ordering #: 0-671-68381-0

Published by Meadowbrook Press, 18318 Minnetonka Boulevard,
Deephaven, MN 55391.

BOOK TRADE DISTRIBUTION by Simon & Schuster, a division of Simon
and Schuster, Inc., 1230 Avenue of the Americas, New York, NY 10020.

89 90 91 92 5 4 3 2 1

Printed in the United States of America.

Contents

Preface

Dear Boss:

Re: **Purpose of this Book**

Most people want a little praise and recognition for their efforts. You're not different. You deserve a pat on the back for the job you do. You face pressures we never know about. You probably even shelter us from a lot of them so we don't have to worry. And when you think we're right, you back us up. We appreciate your support—we really do! We also respect you because you're well intentioned; you sincerely believe your efforts are in the best interest of all concerned.

On a personal level you can be warm and charming. Sometimes you show your warmth simply with your quick smile. Other times you show a genuine appreciation for our effort, whether by your words or by your actions. Believe it or not, we're thankful and want you to succeed. If we didn't, we wouldn't bother writing this book for you.

We believe in you. We believe you can change your management style and become a better boss. Maybe we're wrong and you can't change. Some people just can't. But we give you this book because we *know* you can be a better manager, maybe even a leader.

Now don't get angry at us. Remember, "All great truths begin as blasphemies," as George Bernard Shaw observed. We're well intentioned; we're trying to help you see yourself as we see you. Perhaps you might try thinking of us as modern-day versions of the spirits of Christmas, who showed Scrooge how others viewed him. Initially he became defensive, but the spirits caused him to face reality and then let him decide on the changes he wanted to make. It would be easy for you, too, to become defensive and assume we're wrong. And we might be wrong, maybe completely wrong, in some of our memos. But regardless of how you think you really are, this book shows how *we* see you. We realize that growth is not always easy and seldom fun. But remember, a rut is simply a shallow grave with the ends kicked out. Please climb out of your management-style rut and read this book! It will make your life as boss easier both for you and for us.

If nothing else, humor us. Take a risk and assume we're right as you read these memos. If you do, you'll grow. You might even become a better boss—maybe even *the* better boss we all want.

Unconvinced? Maybe you should be. Clearly you're more successful than we are: you're the boss! So why consider our memos? Perhaps a specific topic might convince you to read on. Have you ever run into resistance to change—you know, where we drag our feet, only half supporting your decision or goals? At times resistance is pretty common around here. Your usual response is to blame us. (And we're usually guilty, too.) But have you ever thought, "There must be a better way"? Well there is! And since you're the boss, the better way starts with you. It's your responsibility to find it. Resistance is a tangled path; untangling it starts with understanding how *you* contribute to it. In fact, your behavior gives us the crutch we lean on to justify our resistance. You'll find partial explanations for our resistance in the memos "Making Decisions" on page 114 and "Resistance to Change" on page 112. If you want to change the outcome, change what you bring to our work relationship, rather than trying to change us.

As Martin S. Davis, Chairman and Chief Executive Officer of Gulf Western Industries, Inc., wrote:

> America's managers have come through economic trials far tougher than they were accustomed to. Along the way they have learned that some old precepts they had abandoned still have validity, while some new approaches have proved fallacious. Regardless of their age or the age of their organizations, they are coming through another stage of corporate maturation. They are experiencing a new self-awareness, and seeking to change about themselves what they recognize needs to be changed.
>
> It is not a painless process, but it is a process that cannot be avoided if there is to be progress.[1]

Don't worry. We bought extra copies of this book, and we're reading ours, too. (We wanted to read it before someone gave it to us!) As you'll see in this book, we're not perfect and we realize it. Sure, we thought about tearing out and giving you just the memos that apply to you. But, instead, we decided you might benefit from the entire book. In the Table of Contents we checked the memos you most need to read, although the other ones might be worth a glance, too.

Most sincerely yours,
Your Employees

P.S. This book expresses our intense feeling regarding some of these issues. At times it may sound harsh, even negative. If it offends you, we are sorry, but please remember that we want you to understand how we think *and* feel.

CHAPTER 1
YOU CAN CHANGE

Dear Boss:

Re: **Bosses Who Grow**

 Your growth will come from applying these memos to *your* leadership style, not from gleefully agreeing with us that your own boss should change. Perhaps your boss should change, too. But as you read this book, remember to ask yourself, "How do these memos apply to me?" If you do, you'll become a boss who grows.

Dear Boss:

Re: Change

　　We're all in the business of change, not maintaining status quo. Whatever we're doing, by whatever means, will be wrong in the future. So we must continually shed our past practices and grow into a new form, with new behavior, if we are to meet the future. As the sign on the desk of an ARCO board member says, "All of business is making changes in anticipation of changes being shoved down your throat."[2]

Dear Boss:

Re: **Choices**

Perhaps the most important thought we would like to share with you deals with choices. When it comes to how you handle your job—the way you manage us—you have choices. You can choose to manage us in a different manner. It won't be easy, and many times habit will cause you to fall back into your old ways. Nevertheless, you can choose how you want to treat us; you can choose how we perceive you. Those choices are yours.

You can't exercise choice by just wishing to change. Wishing is like the lady who rushed up to the famous piano player and said, "I'd give my life to play as superbly as you do." Without hesitation the pianist retorted, "I did." Wishing isn't enough. You must identify those parts of your management style that are weak and change them. That means you must elect different ways of behaving and then behave differently. No easy task, indeed!

Take some topic in this book that you need to change (perhaps one of the topics we checked in the Table of Contents, or some issue that has arisen in your personal life). Examples might include performance reviews, meetings, employee suggestions, or attitudes about ex-employees. You'll know it's the right topic to work on because you'll have rationalization upon rationalization about why you do it the way you do. Once you've identified the topic, ask someone you trust to critique the way you handle the issue.

Next, find another way to handle that situation. (If you find you can't handle the issue any other way, that's

OK. We can't always change. But at least you'll know you *can't* change, not *won't* change.) You might have to go to the library to research the recommended way to deal with the situation. Or, you might try the suggestions in this book. The key is to handle some aspect of your job differently so you can experience *choice* in your leadership style, or at least in some aspect of it. If you succeed and handle some situation differently, you'll know you have choices. You'll know you're not just reacting in some traditional, unchanging pattern.

The choice is up to you. You can change your management style, in whole or in part. When you exercise choice, you enhance your self-image. You grow.

Dear Boss:

Re: **The Success Trap**

"Don't tinker with success." We bet you believe that this axiom is true when applied to your management style. Moreover, we bet you can prove your management style is successful: look how far it's taken you—a lot further than any of us. *You are the boss.* Someone sees you as more competent than any of us to run things around here. Just the fact that you are the boss *proves* you're better. So why should you change? Your success demonstrates conclusively that your management style is the right one.

Agree? If you do, you're caught in the Success Trap. Your past successes have reinforced your management style to the point where you are beyond questioning it. Your style is fine; therefore, any problems of morale and motivation must have another explanation.

Actually, we believe that if it weren't for your management style, you'd be even *more* successful. Have you ever felt you're a better manager than your boss gives you credit for? You are. What holds you back is your style. You see, how you treat us largely determines how we perform. You can trace the principle of "You get what you give" all the way back to the Bible: "For whatsoever a man soweth, that shall he also reap" (1 Cor. 6:7).

Sow a different management style, and you'll reap a harvest of morale and motivation. Just because your present style was successful in the past doesn't mean it's still appropriate. Horse-drawn carts have been around since biblical times, but trucks are better! Your analytical abilities are fine. You understand much about our business. But the way you lead people (or fail to) needs to change.

Just remember that the major cause of failure is success. Success reassures. It makes us less willing to re-examine ourselves. It slows down our growth because we get caught in the trap of our past successes, held in place by inertia. Don't cling to your past successes. They're in the past! Greater successes await you in the future.

CHAPTER 2
TAKING RESPONSIBILITY

Dear Boss:

Re: **Externals vs. Internals**

Psychologists have developed a test that measures a person's locus, or center, of control. The test shows whether people see their world as controlled primarily by themselves or by external factors. Some people find their control within themselves; others find it outside themselves.

This distinction is more than just an academic exercise. People who are controlled by factors outside of themselves are usually "victims" of the world in which they live. They see everything that happens to them—at least the bad things—as the results of forces beyond their control. The world *does* things to these "externals." Those who are "internals," on the other hand, *influence* outcomes; they are initiators, not helpless victims.

To illustrate, let's consider a situation every boss faces from time to time. Assume we have a new employee who has been with us for fifty-eight days, and the probation period is sixty days. This new employee just isn't making it and must be terminated before the sixty days are up. A boss controlled externally will think:

"These kids today don't want to work."

"The personnel department can't hire good people."

"Somebody better improve our training programs."

"I've told that new worker to shape up."

This external boss doesn't take any responsibility for the failure, instead seeing the probationary employee as failing because of forces beyond the manager's control. The boss feels like a victim of outside forces. Thus absolved of any failure, this boss can fire the unacceptable worker with a clear conscience.

A boss controlled internally, on the other hand, will think very differently:

"I needed to spend more time orienting and motivating this new employee."

"If I had checked background references personally."

"I better recheck our new-employee training program."

"Perhaps I should review the accuracy of Personnel's job description."

"With more coaching from me, this new worker might have been a successful performer."

Here the boss takes responsibility for the outcome, assuming that the situation is within his or her own control. This internal boss has an impact on the job setting and is not just a helpless victim like the external counterpart.

In this example both types of bosses end up letting the probationary employee go. So what difference does it make whether you're an internal or an external? Well, which type of manager is most likely to succeed with the employee's replacement? Which boss is acting more responsibly? Shows the better mental health? Has lower stress? Which boss is likely to earn more respect from supervisors, peers, and employees?

Perhaps the truly critical question is, "Which boss will grow?" The first manager, having found external causes for the probationary employee problem, stops looking for other reasons. One solution ends the search for other solutions. Once absolved of failure, this boss feels no need to change or grow.

But the second boss, the one with internal control, assumes at least partial responsibility, which causes him or her to grow by searching for a better approach in hiring new employees.

Dear Boss:

Re: **Luck**

We've observed that the bosses with the most luck are actually the ones who work the hardest. For, in the final analysis, luck is just preparation meeting opportunity.

The more you plan and prepare, the better example you set. The higher your standards, the harder we work. Think about bosses you've had. The ones who set high standards caused you to raise your sights. Bosses with low standards allowed you to cut corners.

When you set a high standard by your example, our success doesn't need to depend on luck.

Dear Boss:

Re: **Can't vs. Won't**

We know this is picky, but some of us find your use of the word "can't" annoying. Many times when we have a suggestion, need a rule bent, or seek some other special consideration, you tell us you can't do anything about it. If you were really unable to do anything about our request, we could accept "can't." But you know and we know that you can almost always do *something* to help. You could, for example, talk to your boss or someone else. Yet you tell us you can't do anything about it.

Here's a simple test: if your life literally depended on doing something about our request, would you still say "I can't help?" If, under such extreme circumstances, you were unable to help, then, "can't" would be the right word. Otherwise, take responsibility for your actions (or inaction) by saying, "I *won't* do anything about your request." You could even soften this harsh-sounding response with a reason. But please stop saying *can't* when you really mean *won't*.

Dear Boss:

Re: **Blind Loyalty to Your Own Boss**

We know your boss expects you to be loyal. Loyalty to your boss makes you a team player, someone your boss finds comfortable to have around. But, do you realize that your blind compliance with your boss's orders carries a high price? Some of us knew you before you were promoted to your present position. You seemed like an OK person! We realize that as your boss's right hand, you get a lot of subtle benefits. But when you blindly support bad decisions by your boss, your credibility with us drops. Too often, rather than stand up for us or disagree with your boss, you comply. Don't get hooked into blind compliance; be your own person. Otherwise, your credibility is shot. Unless your boss is even more insecure than we think, you'll lose credibility there, too, once your boss realizes you're an unthinking robot.

When you have the unenviable task of passing on one of your boss's decisions, even if it's a stupid one, too often you follow through with your task blindly. Being a good subordinate, you don't try to distance yourself from the decision by saying, "This is what needs to be done even though I disagree." Instead—you just implement the order.

Since you don't put distance between you and the decision, however, the order appears to be yours. Or at least you look as though you support it. And when you support stupid decisions, you look stupid. You merge your credibility with that of your boss, which makes sense only if your boss is competent. If your boss isn't, then you appear incompetent, too. We hope your loyalty is worth the price you're paying in credibility and reputation! By the time your boss leaves, your reputation will be shot. No one will consider you for the promotion we suspect you seek.

You're in a double bind: comply and look stupid, or defy and be insubordinate. Perhaps you should jump ship into another department or organization. But that wouldn't be loyal.

What should you do? First, don't blame your boss—that will make you look like a relay station instead of a boss. Second, talk to us about the purpose of the order. We may have some ideas on how to get the task done in a better way. You get the results your boss wants and we feel as though you listen to us. Third, if you lack the authority to modify the order or the approach, still ask us if we have any ideas. If we do, then you have a reason to go back to your boss and say, "One of my people made this suggestion. If we use the employee's idea, this change you want is likely to go much quicker, with less foot dragging now and later."

If your boss has had second thoughts about his idea, he may agree to our approach. If he does not agree, at least he'll know you're not some robot. Then when you come back to us, you can say "I tried." We still won't like the idea, but we'll be a lot more likely to do it right, just to support you for trying.

Dear Boss:

Re: Complaining

Management is difficult. No one ever said getting people to do things would be easy. No one ever promised you a boss who would be considerate, supportive, and effective.

Yet, you act as though the role of manager should be easy. Once you accept—truly accept—that being a manager is difficult, you won't be so upset by our mistakes or the lack of support from your own boss. You'll come to expect and accept problems. And maybe, just maybe, you'll stop complaining about how difficult your lot in life is.

If your job as a boss weren't difficult, it wouldn't need to be done. Or it could be done by someone with fewer skills—and for a much smaller salary.

Besides, your role is *not* to complain. Complaining only pulls down your listeners' morale. Most important, it pulls down your own morale. And once your morale drops, your problems seem even more oppressive. Whatever happened to leadership by example?

You always tell us, "Don't just bring me problems, bring solutions, too." Well, here are our solutions:

1. Quit expecting your role as boss to be easy

2. Understand that problems cause you discomfort

3. Accept that occasional discomfort is part of your job

4. Consider problems as an opportunity to teach us solutions

"Life is a bitch and then you die." Make the most of life by cutting out the complaining.

One of our previous bosses had a positive way to handle unpleasant tasks. He'd introduce them by saying, "Aren't we lucky we get to do this?" We'd all smile, then moan at his exaggerated enthusiasm. Later, when one of us would complain to the others over lunch or on a break, we'd playfully mimic his "Aren't we lucky..." line. It would always get a laugh and break the tension.

When he knew we were going to face a particularly tough week, he'd greet us on Monday morning with "Ah, Mondays. I love them. We have an entire week in which to excel." We'd laugh.

Our point is a simple one: you must be more than a boss, you must also be our cheerleader.

Dear Boss:

Re: Indecision

Indecision plagues us all, especially when we must choose between two unpleasant alternatives. Rather than pick one bad outcome or the other, we do nothing. And often when we have bad news, we don't tell you right away; we become indecisive because we're trapped between the unpleasant task of giving you bad news now, and the fear that if we wait until later, you'll be upset at our delay. Seldom does anyone face the pleasant dilemma of choosing between two positive options, like the donkey in Aesop's fables, who couldn't decide which pile of hay to eat. Choices between positive options don't seem to cause much indecision around here, however.

Indecision often paralyzes us most when the decision is an important one. Often we don't know which alternative is best until we choose one. But the very process of choosing one option often precludes the other, sometimes permanently. So we hesitate, perhaps hiding behind some excuse such as, "Let's get some more data," or "Have we considered all of the repercussions." We need information and reflection to make effective decisions, but let's not mistake careful thought for indecision.

Indecision prevents action, and action is the only basis for success. If you're habitually indecisive, you inject uncertainty into our minds. Your indecisiveness undermines our confidence in your decisions and in you, the decision maker. Our lack of confidence undermines our commitment and success, regardless of which choices you finally make.

One way out of this dilemma is to talk with us. You don't have to tell us you are undecided. Instead, tell us you have some choices to make and want our ideas. Even if we pick the second best choice, our involvement means greater commitment from us. Remember, we can't support what we don't understand. Getting us involved may make the difference in the execution of the solution. Besides, "two heads are better than one."

Dear Boss:

Re: **"I'll Try"**

Have you ever noticed that when you ask one of us to do something, we usually say, "I'll try?" It's such a common response that it often slides past unnoticed. Even you use it when we ask you to do something.

We're writing a memo about "I'll try" because of what the phrase signifies. When people say they'll try, whether it's you or us, they're subtly building an excuse for failure. That's right, failure! All they commit themselves to do is to "try." If they fail, they can still claim they did what they said they would: they tried. Saying, "I'll try" is really not making a commitment to *doing* the request; it's merely showing a willingness to try.

When you say, "I'll try," we feel you're really saying, "I'll try when it's convenient to do so. But I make no guarantees about my success. All I have to do is try, and I'll have fulfilled my promise."

We hope the next time someone around here says, "I'll try," someone else will simply say, "Don't just try, *do* it!"

CHAPTER 3
CHANGING YOUR IMAGE

Dear Boss:

Re: **Attention Getting**

We all have a need for attention, a need to be seen, to feel special and unique. And to ensure that we get enough attention, we all develop strategies to attract it. But someone with an excessive need for attention is often over-compensating for feeling uncertain or inferior. Unfortunately, what seems to happen, at least subconsciously, is that the ostentatious behavior serves to remind them of their uncertainty or inferiority. Street graffiti might be the ultimate example—a painted scream for attention and importance.

In an organization people show their need for attention in many ingenious ways. A common one around here is complaining. Even if the complaints are valid, the excessive complaining might signify that people need more attention. Another way to get attention is to be disruptive. Like children doing something forbidden to get their parents' attention, some people here talk loudly, arrive late, have "accidents," gossip, or find other ways to interrupt whatever's going on. Have you ever noticed a new employee being overly gregarious? Or a long-time worker becoming too assertive after being promoted to a new job, such as supervisor?

What a nuisance! But when you, the boss, are the cause of the disruption, more than productivity is lost. Morale suffers. Your self-confidence looks as if it is evaporating. And we lose confidence in you.

Call attention to yourself if you must; we all need to do it. But do you really need to tell us how important you are? Repeatedly? Disruptively?

The best way we know for a boss to get attention is to brag about *us*. When you tell others about one of us who has done a great job or had some special success off the job, it calls attention to you. The unstated message is "I do a great job picking and motivating people." But, since the message is subtle, you don't look as if you are bragging. And, of course, we feel good about ourselves and you. You win, we win.

Dear Boss:

Re: **Ego**

Self-made billionaires are rare. Sam Walton of Wal-Mart fame is one of them. As he observed, "Ego, in my opinion, is one of the worst things that can happen to a company."[3]

Sure ego has its up side. Bosses with strong egos find failure at anything to be distasteful, so they try harder. That's great. But, when we are asked to pursue a project solely to appease your ego, we often don't give it our best shot. Worse, we may try to subtly sabotage your idea to cut you down to size. We should be more supportive. But, when we see no reason for our efforts, we sometimes assume it's to appease your ego. Let us know why we need to tackle each issue. If the only reason is ego, you may be setting yourself up for a failure that none of us really wants.

Dear Boss:

Re: Failure

When you experience a failure, it affects all of us. You are down and so are we. Your successes are our successes, your failures are ours. Of course, failure hurts. It may even take several days to recover from your emotional reaction. But, consider what happens if you sulk around the office for several days. We all feel depressed, too. As a result, we don't give our best efforts.

No matter whether your failure was an embarrassing mistake your boss caught or a promotion you didn't get, your behavior doesn't cause us to rally around you. Instead, you push us away by your sullen mood, rudeness, or outright criticism of our behavior. And when you push us away, you unintentionally *increase* your chances of failing in the future. We feel rejected so we reject you. Our rejection might take the form of an outright argument or perhaps some subtle omission that will create even more problems for you later on. Usually we show our rejection simply by not doing something that we know we should do but that you didn't tell us to.

And when your peers and your boss see you sulk or lash out at us, what opinion do they form of you? Imagine what they would think if you took the failure in stride, with no emotional swings. Your stature would rise much more quickly than when you show your resentment through words or deeds. Your retaliations only reinforce the failure in your own mind and in the minds of others, while at the same time demonstrating your weakness. As Eric Hoffer, a longshoreman turned writer and philosopher, observed,

"Rudeness is the weak man's imitation of strength." His observation could be broadened to include the words or deeds you use to even up the score.

Second-rate bosses try to place blame or find excuses. Effective leaders accept responsibility for failures, solve the problems their failures cause, and then move on to other tasks. Which would you like to be?

Dear Boss:

Re: Fear

Fear might be the major flaw in most of the bosses we've had. Some feared losing their jobs and fell into the Machiavellian Trap of sabotaging their subordinates. Others merely feared losing control and looking foolish. Still others simply feared making mistakes or losing their turf.

A single thread is woven throughout all workplace fears regardless of their cause: our boss sees us as a threat. We become the villains who covet the boss's job, cause the boss to lose control, make the mistakes for which the boss is held responsible, or fail to defend the department's turf. The boss then sees us not as potential allies, but enemies. Then the boss often takes action to defend against our real and imagined transgressions, often adding to the problem. In the words of an old Estonian proverb, what you are afraid of overtakes you. The very actions intended to alleviate the fear often bring it to life.

The only way out of fear is through it. You must confront it to conquer it. Express your fear; share it with those you trust. Let others help you put it into perpective. Then confront it! Groom a successor, for example. Trust someone with an important task and cut the strings of control. Or give away part of your territorial empire. Once you have met your fear, it will no longer control you. As Ralph Waldo Emerson noted, "He has not learned the lesson of life who does not every day surmount a fear."

No one would ever call you cruel, yet your own reaction to fear can turn our department—or even our entire organization—into a House of Fear. As Bertrand

Russell pointed out, "Fear is the main source of superstition, and one of the main sources of cruelty. To conquer fear is the beginning of wisdom." We wish you the wisdom to avoid making your fears a reality.

Dear Boss:

Re: **How Busy You Are**

    We all need sympathy from time to time, especially when we feel oppressed by our workload. But, consider our perspective when you tell us repeatedly how busy you are.

    Again and again we hear how you have so much to do. Sometimes it seems as though you interrupt your work (and ours) to remind us of your workload. We've observed that you're seldom too busy to tell us how busy you are. And if you have time to lament about it then you really can't be all that busy. Get on with your work and stop interrupting ours. We're busy, too, but we don't take the time to tell you about it.

    What's happening around here is that everyone is starting to moan about how busy they are. We sometimes spend more time talking about our workload than tackling it. We know your workload is a pressing issue, but please don't press it on us.

Dear Boss:

Re: Insecurities

None of us is as self-confident as we'd like to be. We all have insecurities. Yours might not even be worth mentioning, except that you're the boss and *we* have to pay for them!

Without a doubt your major insecurity lies in your need to control. Sure, bosses must retain control over themselves and their people; if they can't, their leadership is questioned and they're replaced. But there are limits! When you try to control every aspect of our performance, we feel you are controlling us so you won't end up looking foolish. Often, we rebel by doing exactly what we are told, whether it makes sense or not. We suspend our common sense. Sooner or later, mistakes occur and you apply even more control so you won't look foolish. This cycle of *control—errors—more control* keeps building until a really big mistake occurs. Then your insecurities lead to blame.

Your insistence on blaming someone else makes you look foolish. We're not stupid! Many times we tell you that a problem is coming, but you don't want to lose face by admitting that your orders are wrong. Instead, you stick to your decision and lose even more face with us (and often with your boss, who doesn't buy your excuses and blaming, either). If you were more secure, you'd admit the error, correct it, and gain stature in our eyes for your self-confidence. If you'd take responsibility for your actions—if you'd admit you're at fault when things go wrong—you'd grow and we'd respect you more. Honesty and accepting responsibility are the keys to greater self-worth and personal freedom. When you have greater self-worth, your self-esteem grows while your insecurities fade.

What makes these insecurities so insidious is that you feel threatened so easily. You often see a simple mistake as a direct affront to you. Then you overreact, all out of proportion to the mistake but probably in proportion to your insecurities. Insisting on always being right is simply overcompensating for your fear of being wrong. If you want to appear confident (and probably improve your actual self-confidence), *risk!* Risk your ego and admit your errors.

When you give us the freedom to make mistakes, we learn from them. We grow. We become better performers, less likely to make mistakes in the future. And, paradoxically, when errors do occur, you appear (and are!) more self-confident if you accept the responsibility, rather than lay the blame.

Dear Boss:

Re: **One-Upmanship**

You're our boss and, as such, you're responsible for the performance *and* satisfaction of our work group. We recognize your need for us to do things better. It's your job to add constructive ideas to our suggestions.

Constructive ideas, however, differ from one-upmanship! If we have an idea, yours is better. If we get a new car, yours is nicer. When we tell a story or a joke, you have to top it. If one of us has a good idea, it becomes yours when you talk to your boss. And when you get a chance to deal with senior management, you forget about our efforts and then tell us (repeatedly!) about your conversation with Mr. or Ms. Big.

The next time you're ready to top one of us, ask yourself why you're doing it. Ask yourself what *we* think you're really doing. Are you showing your superiority or your inferiority?

Often people aren't aware that they are playing the one-upmanship game when they try to top someone's ideas or comments. But, consider how you feel when you deal with someone who always seems to need to one-up you. Like us, you want to avoid dealing with that person. You stop making suggestions. In time, you talk with that person as little as possible. When we meet someone socially who does that, we avoid them. Others do too. The result for them is social isolation. When that occurs at work—when we avoid you—you become insulated from what is really going on. You may even cut yourself off from our ideas.

Dear Boss:

Re: **Hero Stories**

Just a quick note about something you do that drives us crazy: your hero stories. You know what a hero story is; it's one in which you emerged from some situation as a hero. Here are your favorites:

"When I worked at...."

"You should have been there when I told my boss he was...."

We all have our favorite little stories we enjoy telling. And, human nature being what it is, none of us tells stories in which we look like a fool; those stories are easily and best forgotten.

In your case, though, we really get tired of hearing the same old stories. You see, you tell too many of them. And you tell the same ones over and over and over again. You're our boss, so we want to be courteous and listen, but there's a limit! We've concluded that you must have massive insecurities and use these stories to pump yourself up—at least in your own eyes.

You're a nice person; you even tell a good story. But please get some new material—especially a new hero! As one psychologist put it, "If you are saying something about yourself that you said before, stop and say something else."[4]

Dear Boss:

Re: Punctuality

An old wise man one of us knew used to say that there are two arrival times we can choose: early and late. Seldom, if ever, can anyone be precisely on time. Of the two alternatives, considerate people choose early.

As with so many other aspects of work around here, you set the example. When you show up at meetings three, five, or fifteen minutes late, how can you expect us to be punctual or to preach punctuality to our people? Rank might have its privileges, but it also has its responsibilities. And one responsibility of leadership is leading by example. Be on time! And start meetings on time to demonstrate with your actions that punctuality is important.

Dear Boss:

Re: **Optimism vs. Pessimism**

As Shakespeare observed in the play, *Julius Caesar*, "Men at some time are masters of their fates. The fault, dear Brutus, is not in our stars, but in ourselves." The optimist and the pessimist are each right about an equal amount of the time. But optimists have more fun! And when the boss is an optimist, the other workers also have more fun. Optimism sets a more positive, hopeful tone. Sometimes bosses are too insecure to be optimistic because they fear that their optimism will be mistaken for naiveté. And the fear of looking foolish is the biggest fear most bosses have.

Be optimistic. Try to see the positive side of any situation. If you do, you'll convey a can-do attitude that will give us all a reason to be more optimistic. Between optimism and pessimism, which do you think has the best impact on our morale and motivation?

Dear Boss:

Re: **Looking Promotable**

We want to see you get promoted because that promotion will create an opportunity for one of us to move up. We're on your team. So we want to point out some of the things you do that, frankly, hurt your chances for promotion.

First and foremost, stop telling everyone that you want a promotion. Of course you do! Who doesn't? But when you tell people you want a promotion, they become suspicious. They think you're politicking for the job. Even worse, your enemies have plenty of time to subtly sabotage your chances.

Second, you need to look the part. The best advice any of us ever heard was to dress like your boss, not your peers. If your peers wear shirts and ties but your boss adds a sport coat, you need to wear a sport coat, too. If your boss wears a suit, then wear a suit. For people to think of you as promotable, you must look the part.

Third, express a positive attitude. When asked to tackle an assignment, respond with a self-confident smile and "Can do!" Not a disheartened stare at the top of your shoes followed by a meek, "I'll try."

Fourth, make yourself replaceable. That's right, replaceable! You know as well as we do that some people aren't promoted because, when their name comes up for consideration, someone asks, "Yeah, but who'd we get for a replacement?" If you aren't easily replaceable, other people might get promotions simply because they're easier than you to replace. Fair? Of course not! Realistic? You bet.

Fifth, don't become identified with a single job. If you become Mr. or Ms. Shipping around here, it becomes hard for higher-ups to see you doing something else. Express interest in lateral transfers when you know there's an opening; it will show people that you see yourself as broader than your present job. (It will also show that you're willing to move laterally just to help out the organization and get more diverse experience.)

Finally, nothing matters more than how well you do your job. Do it the best you can. And don't forget to let us help you. Making us your allies helps you and it also helps us feel wanted. Besides, creating a high-morale unit can only help your image within the organization. And, even though your public image might not seem like the key to a promotion, it is. Most people are promoted because of what other people think they can do.

CHAPTER 4
EARNING OUR RESPECT

Dear Boss:

Re: **Earning Credibility**

Credibility is tough to earn and easy to lose. And once it's lost, it's virtually impossible to regain. Nothing undermines your credibility faster than dishonesty, no matter whether you're dishonest through bald-faced lies or unfulfilled promises. Perhaps no characteristic of a boss should be guarded more carefully than credibility. You earn it (and get to keep it) when your actions match your words. When a gap exists between your words and your actions, it forms a hole in your credibility.

Dear Boss:

Re: **Keeping a Confidence**

We all want to be trusted. We all want to feel so important that you are willing to confide in us. So when you tell us a secret, no matter whether it's inside information or simple gossip, at first we feel flattered; we're all ears.

But what really happens when you tell us a secret, something that begins with "Don't repeat this..."? Telling us secrets damages your credibility with us. It tells us that you can't keep a confidence. And that makes us reluctant to trust you.

We know that when you share a secret with us, you sometimes hope that we will do the same. But, that approach to finding out what's on the grapevine often backfires. If we share our confidences with you, we announce our inability to keep secrets. Even worse, if you use that information, sooner or later others in the group will figure out who the stool pigeon is. Soon everyone (you included) realizes that this person can't keep a secret. Then trust among all of us drops. Alliances form. Politics replace work as the primary activity around here. Secrets become the local currency, freely bartered for personal gain.

Most important of all, our trust in you drops. We now know you can't keep a secret. Not only do we become reluctant to share information with you, but other people are likely to start spreading disinformation. Lies become mixed with truth. Then resentment focuses on you for encouraging the process with "Don't repeat this." And, since you aren't keeping confidences, why should we.

A sage once observed, "It is better for one to guard a secret than to ask another to do it, too. A secret that is closely guarded is a prisoner. But, once released, the secret makes a prisoner of its guard."

Dear Boss:

Re: Talking About Others

When you engage in negative gossip about other people, it reminds us of the old farm saying, it's hard to spread manure without getting some on yourself.

When you criticize someone in the organization, you send *two* messages: the criticism itself and the fact that you talk about others. When you put down a peer, you usually sound petty and perhaps motivated by jealousy or fear. And when you criticize a superior, you show you're not loyal to either your boss or the organization. You create doubts about *all* the leadership around here, not just your own boss. You see, even if you aim the criticism at a specific superior, you raise the question, "Why are those who are even higher up allowing this to go on?" Soon we question whether *their* superiors are competent. How motivated do you think we are to follow leaders tainted with questions of incompetency? Doubt about the competence of leaders dissolves the psychological bond between leaders and followers. No one benefits.

Criticizing your subordinates raises the nagging question, "What's being said about me when I'm not around?" That question is not idle paranoia. If you talk about one of us, isn't it reasonable to assume you're talking about the rest of us, too?

Likewise, stop making unfavorable comparisons among us! Why tell one of us we're not as good as someone else? Do you really think that motivates us?

Your comparisons do get our attention. But they're also counterproductive. To the poor performers in your comparisons, you're just confirming their inability, which they already know. Your comparison reinforces their already poor self-images. By lowering their self-esteem, you make it *easier* for them to do poorly because they need to expend even less effort to uphold their new, negative self-images. And to the good performers in your comparisons, you're reinforcing their positive self-images—at their co-workers' expense.

Do you think the comparisons encourage people to improve? On the contrary! To avoid standing out, the high performers will usually decrease their efforts so they'll be accepted by their all-powerful peer group. So, unfortunately, your comparisons have the opposite effect you intend: good performers slow down, and poor performers resign themselves to minimal levels of performance.

We all engage in gossip and comparisons about people. But you can be a positive force around here if you will limit your comments to the good things people do. Not only is this true about those you supervise, but it also applies to people in other departments. If you tell us about how bad they are, it doesn't make us better. In time, we start to doubt the competence of the entire organization. We'd much rather think our organization is a well-managed one.

This may sound trite, but if you don't have something good to say, say nothing.

Dear Boss:

Re: **Trusting Us**

Do you ever notice how many subjects around here are considered confidential? We can't be told about sales, backlogs, or—heaven forbid—profits. What are you trying to hide? From whom? We assume you're trying to hide information that would be useful to a competitor. But what would our competitors do even if they had that information? Would it allow them to put us out of business? Or are you simply ashamed of how poorly we're doing?

Perhaps you don't want to let us know out of fear that we'd ask for a raise. But the lack of information creates suspicion among us. We feel that you don't trust us, so we reciprocate by not trusting you. You get trust by giving it! It's that simple. If you don't want our trust, then don't trust us. But suspicion will grow like a weed until it chokes off our loyalty and commitment. Do you want suspicious, untrusting, indifferent employees just because you're afraid a competitor might get some tidbit of information that they could buy from an underpaid accounting clerk, over a couple of beers? Open up the books! Give us a quarterly—or even monthly—briefing about our operation. Make businessmen and businesswomen out of us by educating us about the business.

No, we don't want you to share secrets and confidences. That would undermine our trust in you, as we wrote in the previous memo. What we are asking you to do is open up the flow of information about our business to all of us. We may not own equity in this operation, but we sure have a stake in it. We are devoting a large portion of our lives to this business. Is it unrealistic to want to know how the business is doing? We don't need to know the "secret formula" or even how much you are paid. What we want to know is how we are doing compared to budget, competitors, or last year. Give us feedback about the operation and we'll feel informed and trusted.

Dear Boss:

Re: **Honesty**

Perhaps the best view of honesty comes from Will Schutz, who suggests that we "assess how much honesty the situation will take matter-of-factly and then be slightly more honest than that."[5] Sure, it would be nice if everybody were 100 percent honest all the time. Life would be so much simpler. But total honesty isn't always possible.

Sometimes you're told information that you must keep confidential. Personnel records are one obvious example; another is information about an employee's personal problems. At other times you simply might not know the answer to our questions—maybe no one told you, either. What irritates us is when you're *needlessly* untruthful. When you say, "I don't know," and we know you do, your credibility drops. Why don't you answer us with, "I'm not allowed to discuss it"? Why not tell us, "I can't say"? You don't have to con us. We work for you; we know you. What would impress us is an honest answer. If you don't know, say so. And if you can't tell us, say so.

We would like you to try a new approach for a few days: figure out how much honesty a situation can stand, then be a little more honest than that. It's tough at first, but it gets easier and easier. You'll also find that your life will be far less complicated, and that benefit will reinforce your greater honesty. Being more honest won't be a snap, but with practice, it will be noted and respected.

If you *can't* be honest with us—and we recognize that at times you're sworn to secrecy—tell us. Don't make up some story or excuse. Just level with us.

Dear Boss:

Re: Loyalty

Loyalty is the foundation upon which dedication is built, and dedication must exist if we are to have a high-performing department. But loyalty is earned, it is an exchange. The loyalty one gets depends on the loyalty one gives. As a former president of Yale, Alfred Whitney Griswold, observed: "There are certain things in man that have to be won, not forced; inspired, not compelled. We cannot legislate morality. No, and we cannot legislate loyalty."

Why should you be loyal to us? We seldom show much loyalty to you. Most of us would quit for a slightly better opportunity elsewhere. You might even feel that some of us would stab you in the back if given the chance. Besides, we're paid to do our jobs, which should buy at least our minimum loyalty. So, understandably, you feel little loyalty to us.

If we showed greater commitment to you, to our jobs, or to the organization, your feelings of loyalty toward us would go up. In fact you already feel a high degree of loyalty toward those of us who support your goals and decisions. (Of course, many of us think those people are just brownnosers and your favorites.) But since we show you little loyalty, it doesn't make sense for you to reward us with yours. So you withhold it.

Perhaps we're just waiting for the loyalty to come from you first. Sure, we have to do our jobs. And we know we'd better not be openly disloyal, especially in front of you. But we'll never be enthusiastically loyal toward you unless we receive the same from you. So who should go first? Since you're the boss, you're responsible for what happens (or doesn't happen) around here. Besides, we've never heard that employees should set an example for their boss. We know you agree that good leaders lead by example. Loyalty demands a sense of admiration. How can we admire you if you don't give us loyalty first?

We can almost hear you saying, "Be specific. Give me an example." How about two?

After people quit (not retire or move, but quit), you do a character assassination on them. People who worked hard, maybe for years, are criticized after they're gone. Perhaps you feel betrayed that they left, but why do you create the impression that they were low-lifes? It makes us wonder what you *really* think about us.

Another example is your attitude toward our career development. It's axiomatic that the better we are, the better you look. Now, we realize we must all be responsible for our own career development (which explains why many of us would leave for slightly better jobs). But you do very little to help us develop. Try showing a little more loyalty to us—to our careers. Demonstrate your dedication to our advancement and we'll become loyal to you.

You get what you give. Give us more loyalty. Do it sincerely. Do it long enough for us to notice, and you'll have the most loyal bunch of employees in the organization.

Dear Boss:

Re: **Talk Is Cheap (So Are Promises)**

Henry Ford once observed that "you can't build your reputation on what you're going to do." Your promises to get us raises, or get authorization to hire more people, or get new equipment are just that—promises. At first they sound good; they even give us hope for the future. We walk out of your office believing that things will change because we *want* to believe. By making promises, you tap our desire to believe in you and our wish for things to get better. But sooner or later we all are judged on what we accomplish.

So promise us only what you are certain will happen. Spare us your hopes and wishes until they take firm root in reality. Otherwise your promises become lies, and lies—even well-intentioned ones—cast a dark veil over your integrity.

A hundred kind refusals are better than one broken promise. It's better to refuse our requests than to promise us something you can't deliver. Undelivered promises are seen as lies, lies that undermine your credibility and our pride in you as our boss.

When your promises are not fulfilled—even if they're beyond your control—we lose faith in you. Maybe your own bosses don't realize how important it is for you to save face and follow through on your promises. Maybe they think that you aren't important and that we matter even less. We don't know what either they or you think. All we know is that, too often, you make promises that go unfulfilled. Talk is cheap. So let's see some action on your promises.

Otherwise, it might turn out that Henry Ford was wrong: maybe you *can* build a reputation on what you're going to do. You sure are building a reputation with us— one that says you're all talk and no action. Instead, promise us less than you will provide and we will be pleasantly surprised. Our opinion of you will change to "a boss who delivers."

Dear Boss:

Re: Admit Your Mistakes

Have you ever wondered how we feel when you admit a mistake? The statement, "I made a mistake," is the shortest path to respect. Just admitting you erred shows you're self-confident because only self-confident bosses can freely acknowledge their errors. Once you admit a mistake, all the time and effort you'd normally devote to proving that it *wasn't* a mistake is freed to help you avoid future ones.

Besides, if we see you're willing to admit mistakes, we know your other decisions must be right—if they weren't, you'd admit the mistakes and correct them! Your credibility goes up. And since it's safe for you to admit your mistakes, we can admit ours, too. If you tolerate honest mistakes then we all can take greater risks. The willingness to try and risk making mistakes makes bureaucratic hardening of the corporate arteries less likely. Experimentation can grow, even flourish. And you'll gain our respect.

Dear Boss:

Re: **Pitching In**

What impact does it have on us, your employees, when you literally roll up your sleeves and help us do our jobs? We know you're not paid to do our jobs. We also know that, considering your salary, it's not economical for the organization to pay you to do our work. And we understand that when you help us do our jobs, with your own hands, you're neglecting more important things. We know all that. But does your pitching in have any benefits?

Yes! Pitching in shows us you *care*. It shows you don't feel you're too important to come down to our level. We know our work is not always glamorous and might even be boring. But by pitching in you tell us we matter.

Now don't just rush out of your office and roll up your sleeves right now. Pitching in just for the sake of pitching in, when we're not behind, is unnecessary and unwanted; you'd just get in our way. But when we're behind because of absences or rush orders, feel free to help out. We'll appreciate and respect you for it.

CHAPTER 5
OPENING LINES
OF COMMUNICATION

Dear Boss:

Re: **Improving Communication**

Communication is the lifeblood of any organization. How well we send and receive messages goes a long way to determine how well we perform. Would you like to improve communication among us? Why not simply ask us in for a meeting on communications? Just ask, "What should we do to improve communications?"

After our astonishment wears off, you'll get a series of reactions. The general response will be to test you to see whether you're sincere. Unfortunately, the only way to test your sincerity is to ask for something—perhaps some information. Then we'll watch what you do. If you make a sincere, successful effort to give us that information, we'll start to believe you're sincere. After several more tests we'll slowly lower our guard. Our request might be for previously confidential information about sales, projections, and future plans. If you don't trust us with that information, why should we trust you and communicate? If all you really want is for us to listen to you better, without your really listening to us, then your attempt to improve communications is a sham.

With better communication comes better understanding and greater effort. But, like so many other aspects of management, communication must be managed with the goal of improving it. If communication is the lifeblood of the organization, its improvement will add energy to the organization.

Dear Boss:

Re: **Listening**

Schools and seminars teach us how to read and write, even how to give a speech. But few of us are trained to listen. Also, living in a world full of too many sounds, we teach ourselves to turn off most communications and ignore much of the available information. You're no different from the rest of us. We know you're too busy to take a full course in listening. Besides, you probably already know about active listening, which requires you to pay careful attention, take notes, and ask questions. Nevertheless, we'd like to acquaint you with one technique popular among counselors, particularly marriage counselors.

When a woman seeks marriage counseling (and women are often the first to seek this type of help), the counselor usually is of little help to her after a few meetings, since the problem involves *both* the husband and the wife.

If the woman can convince the husband to attend counseling, then the fuss begins. Each one tries to convince the marriage counselor that he or she is right, and would the counselor please straighten out the other one? Of course the counselor can't pick sides. The result is a flood of recriminations screamed and shouted from both sides. Neither the husband nor the wife is listening.

To remedy the situation the counselor calls a truce and sets forth the following guidelines: only one person may speak at a time. No interruptions are allowed. After the speaker finishes, the listener summarizes the speaker's words without refuting any of the speaker's points. The listener is not required to agree, merely summarize accurately. Then they reverse roles, with the rebuttal and recriminations flowing in the opposite direction, while the other person listens and summarizes.

In time, they learn to listen.

We aren't married, but using this method would help you improve your listening skills. And, more important, we would sense your greater interest in us because your body language, understanding, and attention would improve. If you listened carefully enough to summarize what we say, we'd know you care. In return we'd care more, too. But the caring must start with you.

Careful listening improves your grasp of the content of our message, but what about the feelings behind the message, where the true meaning often lies? Careful, active listening *does* increase your chances of hearing our latent feelings. But if you really want to sense both content and feelings, you'll need to work on some other skills, too.

The key to hearing both the content and the feelings starts with you. You must acknowledge and respond to the feeling side of communications, rather than just dealing with the fact, the content. Now, sometimes you barely look up from your desk when we walk into your office, which means you don't see our body language. Develop the habit of making eye contact so we'll feel less intimidated. If we're less intimidated, we'll be more likely to open up and tell you how we feel. Then, if you acknowledge and validate our feelings, we'll feel affirmed—we'll feel safer and more willing to share our opinions and feelings, openly. You'll get more—and better—content.

Simple acknowledgement works well: "Gee, you

must have put in a lot of hours compiling this information," or "You should feel proud of this report. It's a superb job." If you see that someone is nervous or distraught, affirm the obvious: "This must be an upsetting experience for you." Make contact with the *feeling* side when someone talks with you. If you do, you'll seem—and you'll be—more accessible. People will feel as though you care about them as people. Consider the saying, "We have two ears; one to hear the content and one to hear the feelings within every verbal communication." Once you hear the other person's feelings, affirm them by acknowledging them openly. If you ignore our feelings, we'll hide them. But then we'll hide the content, too. You'll silence both.

By stifling communications, you won't create enthusiastic supporters. By not listening carefully enough to summarize our messages, you'll miss their content. And by not affirming our feelings, you'll lead us to withdraw them—*all* of them, including our loyalty, eagerness, and motivation. As John, Viscount Morley of Blackburn, the English statesman, observed in the last century, "You have not converted a man because you have silenced him."

Our organization, like most, values logic and content. But real people have feelings. To ignore feelings is often to ignore an important part of our communications. When you read our memos or hear our comments, ask yourself, "What are the underlying emotions?" You'll get a better picture of what we're really communicating.

Dear Boss:

Re: **Attitude Surveys**

Why can we afford a small army of accountants, but we can't afford an attitude survey to measure people's feelings? Are figures really more important than people? Do dollars mean more than attitudes?

Attitude surveys reveal what people think and feel about the organization and their boss. Sometimes the results are complimentary to a manager, sometimes they are critical. But complimentary or not, we can make this a better place to work by systematically learning what people think and feel. We can aim training and coaching at individual strengths and weaknesses, rather than taking our usual shotgun approach. And more important, we can make promotion decisions that reflect people skills *in addition to* technical ability or bottom-line results. Once we sense improvements in our jobs and job environment, our attitudes will become more positive. Morale will go up.

All these benefits of attitude surveys don't just happen, however. They require further action. You'll need to give us feedback about the survey results, even air any unpleasant results. Then you'll need to implement follow-up plans that address our concerns.

Following up on the survey will demonstrate management's commitment to the human side of the business. And you can reinforce that commitment, year after year, by annually applying the attitude survey and follow-up plans. Unfortunately, your bosses probably say they already know what the problems are. And they do. What they lack is an overall reading of our feelings about their leadership style. "We know what the problems are" is an excuse for inaction. Or more likely it's a sign that senior managers fear how they might appear. They don't recognize that favorable survey results only reinforce past behavior; negative results suggest new actions and directions. What we don't understand is if they don't know what the problems are, why don't they run a survey to find out? If they already know, why don't they fix them?

If managers fear the results of an attitude survey, treat each manager's results as confidential, so neither bosses nor peers will learn about the results. Each manager can use the time before the next survey to follow up and improve attitudes. Then they'll have nothing to fear. But let's at least make a start! Creating an open, healthy, positive work environment must begin somewhere.

Imagine what this place would be like five years from now if each year we reduced the causes of dissatisfaction. Discontent would decline; motivation would increase because the employees would believe that the management really cares. The process would release pent-up frustrations, and the release would be emotionally cathartic. If the survey were repeated year after year, you and the other bosses would demonstrate your sincerity about making this a better place to work. And repeating the survey would show that it's not just another quick fix that fixes nothing and is quickly forgotten. Instead you'll know how people really feel—the same people who produce those financial results the accountants continually survey.

Remember, what's really important is *not* our current attitudes. It's whether we feel this place is getting better or worse.

Dear Boss:

Re: Feelings

People in organizations like to play a big game called "We're All Logical." Most of the time we do interact in logical ways. By focusing on the most logical way to do things, however, we neatly sidestep feelings. And yet we all know that motivation and dedication depend on how we feel.

No, we're not suggesting that our organization should be run on the whims of emotion. What we're pointing out is that in our efforts to be logical we deny the importance of feelings. Sometimes we say it's not professional to let our feelings enter into our decisions. We might as well say it's not human, too! Unfortunately, many men have been raised in a John Wayne mind-set that views feelings as a sign of weakness. Besides, most men were trained to suppress their feelings early on by well-intentioned parents who told them big boys don't cry. The message was obvious: men aren't supposed to express their emotions.

Unfortunately, women, too, are caught up in the mind-set of suppressing emotions at work. First, expressing emotions is considered unprofessional. Second, in a typical, male-dominated organization like ours, a woman who expresses her feelings risks being labeled "too emotional." That tag can arrest her future career advancement. Her solution? Act unemotional.

But why do we play this game in the first place? Clearly, all the major decisions we make are emotional ones. Want proof? Consider the major decisions you've made in your life: marriage, children, divorce, and careers. Were these logical decisions or were they really emotional decisions painted with a thin coat of rationalizations called reasons or logic?

Only decisions we don't care about can be purely logical. And if we don't care, if we don't have involvement in our decisions, we probably won't ever be passionate enough to attain excellence. Feelings fuel our passion to do our best. (Perhaps we suppress the emotional side of decision making to avoid being in contact with our feelings. That way we don't need to take responsibility for our behavior.)

All we're suggesting with this memo is that you check out how we *feel* about a decision in addition to what we *think*. Our thinking might well agree with yours because your logic is usually very good. But probe our feelings. See if we're on the same emotional wavelength. If we're not, making some minor adjustments might bring us all together on the same logical and emotional frequencies. Otherwise, the logic-based decision might fail or be retarded needlessly. We might understand what you want, but we may not appreciate it.

Dear Boss:

Re: Oasis and Fortress Management

An advertising campaign for AT&T's long distance service carried the theme, "Reach out and touch someone." Not only is that a catchy way to sell long-distance telephone service, it's also a good way to manage people.

The era of the executive oasis is over. An opulent office sends a message of power and waste. The power implications create an invisible, but real, wall between you and us. And it's hard for us to believe that costs and productivity matter when senior executives have lavish offices. So project a spartan, lean-and-mean image.

At other levels in this organization the offices might not be opulent, but they still project an image that prevents contact between their occupants and the rest of us. They're office fortresses. The managers who occupy them use their secretaries and doors to ward off the casual, drop-in meetings that keep the lines of communication open. They foster formality, not performance.

Contrast these oasis- or fortress-like arrangements with those of Japanese managers, who push their desks up against those of their subordinates. Or consider the managers at Hewlett-Packard who manage by wandering around, or their counterparts at IBM who troll for open doors. How can you or the other managers be sensitive to our needs if you're hiding in some well-guarded fortress or intimidating oasis? At Intel the offices do not have doors. Employees hold private meetings in conference rooms. Secretaries do not act as guards at Intel, either. Open offices mean open communications.

Dear Boss:

Re: **Open-Door Policy**

When knocking down walls to create an open office isn't practical, many companies use an open-door policy. An open-door policy sounds like a good idea because it is implemented to foster open communications. But, have you ever seen an open-door policy that really works? An open-door policy requires us to go into your office, bother you, and take our chances on how you'll react. Going over your head and using your boss's open-door policy is doubly dangerous. The result? We don't use the open doors and the lack of complaints creates the mistaken impression that everything must be OK, more or less.

The only open door that works is one where the *boss* gets up and goes through the door. Seek us out. Engage us in conversation on our own turf. Show genuine concern about our problems. Follow-up actions show your concern more effectively than words. Realize, too, that many of our concerns will seem petty and self-serving to you. But if you take action on these issues, you'll earn our respect.

Once you demonstrate your care for us, we'll do the same for you. Soon you'll notice that we're bringing you ideas to improve productivity and quality. And we'll tell you about ways to save money. But first you must show your concern for us by finding the time to listen and the energy to follow through on our problems. None of this will happen unless you get up, go through the door, and seek us out. Call it "management by wandering around," as they do at Hewlett-Packard, or "trolling for open doors," as they do at IBM. But please *do* it!

Dear Boss:

Re: **Resentments**

Have you ever noticed how resentment can eat at you for days, weeks, and sometimes longer? Resentments—regardless of how they form or why we have them—are our most important form of unfinished business. Sometimes you can't do anything about the cause of a resentment. But we've found that if we clear the air by expressing the resentment and our reasons for it, then the resentment's hold on us weakens. If we can express that resentment to the person who triggered it, we're often able to set it free.

We're not naive enough to think all resentments can be expressed, especially to a boss. First, expressing personal resentments isn't always easy. Second, expressing them to a boss might simply engender more resentment on both sides. But expressing them can be so liberating!

We can't advise you to express to your own bosses all the resentments you might have toward them. But we hope that from now on, you'll allow us to express ours to you so we can all get on with our work, free of the internal gnawing of unexpressed resentments.

Dear Boss:

Re: Help and Understanding

Have you ever heard someone say, "I need your help and understanding"? It sounds so much like a cliché, we hardly notice when someone says it. What we hear is only the request for help. Understanding is so rare that some of us don't even bother asking for it anymore. Instead, we just ask for help.

We employees have hopes and fears, just as you do. All of us have felt rejected. And rejection hurts! So we ask only for help because we're more likely to get that. Then, when we get it, we feel hurt that we didn't also get the understanding we really wanted. We don't act very grateful for the help we got. We might even get angry, though not always to your face, because you showed no sympathy for our feelings; you gave us no understanding, only help.

When we seek help, remember that we also want your understanding, your sympathy, and your appreciation. Make us feel valued and we'll work better and harder. You could keep waiting for us to work harder before you reward us with your caring, but how far has that approach taken us?

W. Somerset Maugham put it slightly differently: "People ask you for criticism, but they only want praise." We might ask only for your help, but we really need your understanding, too.

CHAPTER 6
COMMUNICATING CLEARLY

Dear Boss:

Re: **Communication: Content vs. Process**

All communication has two sides: the content and the process. The content is *what* you say—the words you choose, whether written or spoken. It's the message you *intend* to send.

The process, however, is *how* you say the message, and it carries its own meaning. If you tell us, "It's hot!" while wrapping your arms around your chest and shivering, the process outweighs your words. We get a different message from the one you intended. In this example the nonverbal information carries more meaning; the medium *is* the message. The process sends a message you didn't consciously intend.

Too often, the focus of a communication is the content. We tend to think about what someone said, not paying enough attention to how they said it. You would be a more effective communicator if you also would give consideration to how the message is coming across. Could you say it in a more understanding way? It's not just a matter of whether we understand the communication. How we feel about it is also important. More sensitivity to the process—body language, tone, and words—will make us more receptive and you a better boss.

Dear Boss:

Re: **What You Don't Tell Us**

Sometimes no message is a message. When we are not informed about different aspects of the business, we sometimes assume they're not important. For example, if the people in the warehouse are seldom told about breakage they don't worry about it because it must be unimportant.

What you don't tell us also sends a message. If you don't tell us, for example, what happens to quality, productivity, customer satisfaction, costs, scrap, or absenteeism, your lack of communication carries its own message. And if you wait until one of the areas of concern goes haywire before you tell us of its importance, we wonder why you didn't give us the actual figures as we went along so we could both see and fix the problem. No matter why you don't tell us about these issues, your lack of communication sends a message you probably don't intend: our role in these measures of success is unimportant, which means *we're* unimportant. And if we're unimportant, we don't need to worry about our contribution. Is that what you intend?

Of course not. You want us to be concerned about our performance. You can heighten our concern with feedback. Remember, people do what is inspected, not expected. When we get feedback, we feel you are concerned enough to inspect our work.

Dear Boss:

Re: **Defining Relationships**

The core of your job is managing the myriad relationships around you. In fact management scholars used to argue that the number of subordinates a boss could manage was limited to six or seven people. But regardless of the number of relationships you face, you can define each relationship to be whatever you want.

Unfortunately, most of the bosses we've had never defined the relationships they wanted with us, so the relationships took form without any blueprints. Most bosses define the relationships from day to day, even from hour to hour, in whatever way seems to meet their needs. On some days they want employee ideas, on some days they don't. At some hours they expect employees to show initiative, at some hours they don't. Then they wonder why we seem indifferent about quality, productivity, and our relationship with our boss.

We're not sure how you've defined the types of relationships you want with us. Maybe you have them clearly thought out. If you do, share them with us! If we all had the same vision of what we wanted our relationship to become, that vision would serve as the blueprint for our future behavior.

Remember, you can define any relationship to be anything you want. It might not become what you seek, but it's more likely to if you define it clearly. A simple way to define these relationships is to ask each of us to write a description of how we see our job, then discuss it with us individually.

Dear Boss:

Re: **Double Messages**

We all send double messages that confuse our listeners. Perhaps pointing out the most common ones will help:

What you say		How you respond
"I want your ideas"	vs.	"Your idea is not well thought out; come back when it is."
"I want to improve communications around here."	vs.	"I don't have time to talk to you now."
"What's bothering you?"	vs.	"I can't help you."
"Let me help you."	vs.	"Bring me solutions, not problems."

What's the real message? We only have one way to tell: we watch your behavior, which speaks louder than your words.

The match between our words and actions is crucial. If we say one thing but respond in a different manner, we send a mixed message. Periodic meetings about communications, even attitude surveys, might help identify the specific double messages we hear. You may even want to raise the question of what double messages are common at our next staff meeting. Perhaps you could ask each of us to identify the one that is most common.

Dear Boss:

Re: **Defensiveness**

Have you ever noticed that when you're right and you accuse someone else of being wrong, the other person gets defensive?

Defensiveness is a normal reaction. When you point out our errors, we typically react defensively. Either we deny outright what you're saying, or we agree with you but defend ourselves with excuses and rationalizations. When you say we're wrong about something particularly important, our defensive reactions are even more energetic and vocal. Often you can tell whether you're right just by our reaction. If we overreact, you're almost certainly correct, since we're probably protesting so strenuously to convince ourselves. As Shakespeare observed, the guilty tend to overdo it: "The lady doth protest too much, methinks." If your accusations were totally false, our denials would be far less emotional.

Yet we find that you, too, are overly defensive. When we do what you tell us and it turns out that your directions were wrong, for example, you protest (too much, we think). Your defensiveness reaffirms our conviction that you're wrong and we're right. Our conviction, however, does us little good if you still insist that we—not your directions—are at fault. You do, after all, have the power to quash our protest.

But what would happen if you admitted your errors when you made them? First, our respect for you would go *up*. Yes, up. Your admission would show us that you're self-confident enough to admit your mistakes. And if you followed it with a request for our help, you'd be more likely to gain our commitment than you would by your strenuous denial.

But, what about those cases where you really believe you're right and we're wrong? Here you need to rely on your feelings. When you catch yourself strongly denying some accusation (such as "We did what you told us to do"), check out your feelings. If you feel very upset with us, ask yourself why. Is it because we're right and you don't want to admit it to yourself? That's the Gut Test. It will tell you the truth. If we're right, acknowledge that and seek our help. If we're wrong, show some compassion. Don't let your anger cut the threads that bond you and us into an effective work team.

Dear Boss:

Re: **Perception vs. Reality**

One of the toughest lessons for any boss to learn is that you *don't* manage reality. You might think you do, but you don't. What you manage is people's perceptions of reality.

Your greatest frustration is when you know that the real situation is different from what others see. Trying to get others to see your reality is difficult, if not impossible. Have you ever said to someone, "No, you're wrong"? Do most people respond, "Ah ha! You're right. Now I see the light! Thanks so much for telling me I was wrong"? Hardly! People won't see your reality just because you tell them theirs is wrong. Instead they work even harder to convince you of theirs.

What happens? Usually, an argument. If the people you're trying to convince have less power, as do subordinates, they might back down, look at their feet, and say they agree with you. Of course as they walk away they're really reminding themselves you're wrong.

So what are you to do? Think of reality as the *other* people's perceptions. Psychologists have a dictum that's appropriate here: start where the person is. Psychologists don't tell someone who comes to them with a problem, "You're wrong." They don't say, "You shouldn't feel that way." Instead, they accept where the person is and go from there.

We know you're not a psychologist—you're a boss. You have neither the background nor the time to be a psychologist. But if someone has an inappropriate perception, what do you do? Trying to pry people away from their perceptions with forceful arguments won't work because the harder you push, the tighter they cling.

Accept their misperception. If you can, tell the employees you know how they feel, so they don't have to argue the point to get you to listen. Point out that others have felt the same way until they saw the benefit or wisdom of looking at reality differently. You validate their feelings by admitting that others have felt the same way—perhaps even give an example.

This approach will allow the employees to loosen their grips on their position. They don't have to cling to their beliefs for fear they'll lose ground in the argument. Instead you're providing them with allies, others who have felt the same way. Once the employees aren't clinging tenaciously to their beliefs, you might be able to introduce an example, an analogy, or the clear-cut facts that helped convince you or others, sliding them between the people and their beliefs.

You might not hear instant agreement. But the *feel-felt-found* approach probably offers your best chance of getting people to accept another viewpoint. Tell them you truly understand how they *feel*. Remind them that others *felt* that way, too, until they *found* some new fact that altered their perspective. Once you do that, stop! Let both viewpoints coexist. If yours is really closer to reality, the other perception will fade. In time the people might even become converts, or even zealots, for your viewpoint because giving up their old perspective creates a void; your ideas present an alternative to which they can cling.

Dear Boss:

Re: Validating People

Too often bosses work at changing people, not validating or confirming how they feel. You might find it hard to accept, but you can't change most people unless they feel validated. You see, when you want to change us, you want us to behave in a different way. Logic might say all you have to do is tell us what you want done. And that *is* all you have to do unless we're emotionally tied to the old way. If we are then even the best logic and the most forceful motivational approaches will probably fail. Sure, you can order us to change, and we will—reluctantly. Our reluctance will act as an anchor, slowing, maybe even stopping, the change.

If, however, you validate us, we'll be more willing to change. Have you ever been in a heated discussion with people whose opinion you were trying to change? The more you argue for your way, your idea, the more insistent they become that their veiwpoint is right. The more you push, the more they cling to their ideas. It's a common reaction. As the argument continues, everyone's emotional investment in their position grows, making changes even less likely because of the emotional cost. But what if you smile and say, "I see your point," or "You know, you might be right," then they're free to loosen their grips on their own position. By agreeing with them you simply validate their viewpoint. Once you validate it, their need to defend it drops. And as it drops, they're more willing to see the wisdom of your thinking. They might not suddenly turn around and agree with you, but they're now free to *choose* between their argument (which now all of you accept) and yours.

So don't try to change people, validate them! When you do, it frees them from clinging tightly to their position.

William James, the Harvard psychologist whom many view as the founder of psychology in the United States, observed, "I now perceive one immense omission in my psychology—the deepest principle of human nature is craving to be appreciated." When you validate us, we feel appreciated.

Affirm our existence by telling us what we do well. Let us know you appreciate us. Tell us why you respect us. Those affirmations help us feel validated, help us feel able to change and take on the tasks before us.

Dear Boss:

Re: **The Tyranny of Meetings**

We all want to do a better job, but, it's impossible if we're tied up in unproductive meetings. As it now stands, however, we're afraid to skip a meeting because we might miss something or because our absence would look bad. So off we go to still another meeting.

Here are some ideas to reduce the tyranny of meetings:

1. Substitute a memo (handwritten, with space for a reply) if it will replace a meeting. You'll probably get a quicker and better response than if you schedule, hold, and follow up on a meeting.

2. Make "No comment" an acceptable response. Our meetings drag on because we all think we should say something about each item. So we make a lot of time-wasting, gratuitous comments ("I agree with you"; "Let me know if I can help"; "Notify me of the next meeting").

3. Make attendance optional. We don't all need to attend. Besides, with fewer of us there, the meeting will move more quickly. So we'll stay informed, have a secretary distribute the minutes within one-half working day. (Be sure the action items are marked, perhaps with an asterisk.)

4. Never have a meeting without a pre-posted agenda. It will help keep the meeting from wandering off on tangents that we're neither prepared to discuss nor interested in discussing. If

you send the agenda around in advance, you'll be better organized and so will we. We'll be more likely to remember the meeting; the agenda is a not-so-subtle reminder. Furthermore, we'll be more likely to bring the right folder. Besides, an agenda gives us a stated purpose and goals so we can gauge our progress during the meeting.

5. Can we stop passing out supposedly important (and usually voluminous) documents at meetings? When we get a report, fat or skinny, curiosity drives us to thumb through it. We're distracted from the meeting and usually end up asking redundant questions about items that were covered while we looked at the document. Besides, once we've thumbed through it, we feel as though we've looked at it, so it never gets the thorough attention it deserves. Either pass out documents before the meeting, with the agenda, or make them available at the end.

6. Do we need our regular, standing meeting? It's a tradition and it does serve some good purposes. But do we always need it? Many of us scurry around trying to find something to say so we can contribute. The result? We exchange a lot of marginal information just so we can have a meeting at some fixed interval. Don't misunderstand us. We know meetings are more than the formal exchange of information. Networking with our peers is crucial. Many times the coffee breaks during meetings turn into quick, stand-up meet-

ings for smoothing over personal relations, setting up golf games, and catching up on other personal items. The period before and after meetings also provides this personal time, too. (And, of course, these ad hoc meetings get business done, as well.)

7. Start our meeting precisely on time. Once we know you'll be punctual, we'll be on time, too.

8. Announce an ending time so we can plan our other work. Besides, as every psychologist knows, a definite ending time will put gentle pressure on us to get on with the real business of the meeting. And you, as chair of the meeting, can say, "Time is running out," to refocus the group on the agenda.

9. Don't pretend that we're meeting so we can jointly make a decision you've already made. Not only is that a waste of time, it also undermines our contribution when you really need it. The message you've given us is that you don't need us.

10. Remember to call for a break at the first sign that physical, mental, or emotional discomfort may be preventing us from focusing our full attention on the issues.

11. Follow these guidelines. If you don't, we won't!

Meetings consume our most valuable resource—time. We will appreciate anything you can do to speed them up or reduce their frequency.

CHAPTER 7
FEEDBACK ON OUR
PERFORMANCE

Dear Boss:

Re: Management by Exception

Feedback on our performance is crucial. We need it to do a better job. Often bosses operate on a management-by-exception approach. It saves time. But, carried to an extreme, it deprives us of feedback. Consider this frequent comment: "If you don't hear from me, you're doing OK."

Since the only time we hear from you is when we've made some mistake, our interactions with you are predominantly negative. Sure, you can be jovial when we pass in the hallway. But when it comes to interacting over our jobs, there's either a void or criticism.

Consider the perspective of typical new recruits, who start out full of enthusiasm and the desire to do things right. When they finish a task for the first time, the newcomers see only the silent void of no criticism—not even a word of approval or recognition. They try again, and again there's silence. A third, fourth, even fifth time will come and go and the newcomers see only your silence, your management by exception. Even the dullest new employees soon realize that good performance earns no rewards over mediocre performance. Fearful that the newcomers' good performance might show us up, we old-timers place subtle pressure on them to perform at an average level. Since peer acceptance is crucial and extra effort earns no approval or recognition, the peer pressure wins while you wonder what happened to the newcomers' enthusiasm. Soon, your management by exception has created still more mediocre employees who are protected by everyone else's mediocre performance.

You lose. We lose. The only winners are our better-managed competitors. None of us enjoys the resulting mediocrity—and neither do you. Soon our jobs become just mindless ways to spend forty hours a week.

Our enthusiasm will never be as great as yours. You really can't expect us to be *more* enthusiastic than you, can you? And if you hide your appreciation, approval, recognition, and enthusiasm behind "If you don't hear from me, you're doing OK," we'll hide behind our apathy. You can break through our apathy with the battering ram of recognition. Let us know when we are doing a good job. We'll repay you with greater motivation.

Dear Boss:

Re: The Power of Rewards

People do what gets rewarded. But that principle works two ways. First, if there are behaviors you want from us, reward them. With money? Sure! But if the budget won't allow that, use time off, simple prizes, or old-fashioned recognition. Just be sure to reward the behaviors you want to see more often.

Second, when you see behaviors you *don't* want, remember that they often continue because they, too, are rewarded—albeit unintentionally. People seldom take risks around here, for example, because risk-*avoiding* behavior is rewarded. People who risk and fail are punished. Stop rewarding risk avoidance and see what happens!

Dear Boss:

Re: **Blame vs. Consequences**

Every time a problem occurs, we have two choices: we can look backward to the causes or forward to the consequences. Around here, so much effort is placed on finding blame that most of us end up walking backwards, trying to cover our tracks with memos and other documentation to prove our innocence when things go wrong. And, since we devote so much energy to covering our tracks, we shortchange the organization on our efforts to make a project succeed. All because, around here, achieving success is less important than avoiding blame.

Perhaps worse than the cover-your-ass syndrome, just imagine the impact of faultfinding on initiative. If someone champions an idea and it fails, blame rains down on its originator. The result? More and more creativity must come from the top down. Why should we risk the blame that follows a bad idea? Unless your bosses are real dummies, sooner or later they're going to ask, "Why do all the good ideas in your department come from you? Can't you stimulate your people to unleash their creativity?" Then you'll mount a big push for creative ideas. At that point your bosses will find out you can't stimulate innovation, just blame and memos to the file.

Don't misunderstand us. We know you need to determine who's responsible for problems. But fixing responsibility doesn't *solve* a problem, it just delays looking for solutions. So the next time a problem arises, focus on its implications. What needs to be done? How can we save the day? Then, if you must, look for the culprit. Don't look

for the wrongdoer first and let the problem grow worse.
A mistake can be the basis either for punishment or for learning. As our boss you have choices in how you treat our errors. If you punish us, we'll become cautious, unwilling to take risks for fear of incurring punishment if we make a mistake. But if you use our mistakes as an opportunity to coach us, we'll grow—and so will our loyalty, motivation, and morale.

Dear Boss:

Re: **Performance Reviews**

Do you like to give performance reviews? We sure don't like getting them! And that's too bad. We work hard, so performance reviews should make us feel good about ourselves and revved up to perform even better. But they don't. Instead we leave performance reviews feeling browbeaten, even dejected. Often we feel as though all our hard work and effort since the last evaluation have counted for nothing, and all that you remember is our mistakes. It often takes a few days before we even feel like working again. Those of us who are immature even try to get even by not working hard—which only reinforces your assessment.

Don't misunderstand. We need to be told where we're falling down. We all want to improve. We really do! But when you tell us, do it in an uplifting way that motivates us, not in a way that makes us feel next to worthless.

In talking among ourselves, we've spotted some patterns. Perhaps the most damning is that we don't know what we're supposed to do! We know what we're *not* supposed to do; you usually make that very clear. In fact most of each review session centers on what we did wrong. Sure, cover what we did wrong. But that's not enough. Help us understand specifically what we're supposed to do. Describe clearly the attitudes you want us to hold. Even better, define the behaviors we should exhibit. Teach us how we should handle situations. If we don't know how to perform, whose fault is it?

Another pattern—different, but just as bad—is that you do all the talking for the entire review session. Don't lecture us! Tell us what we need to know and then listen.

Sure, you'll hear us make a lot of defensive statements. "Yes, but..." is probably our most common reply when you point out our errors. When you hear us defending our behavior, you undoubtedly get frustrated. We must seem so hell-bent on defending our egos that you know we're not really listening to what you say. Just realize that if we're defensive, it means we feel we're being attacked.

Perhaps you could change your approach so we would feel less attacked. How can you change? Instead of telling us how we fouled up, start by admitting that perhaps *you* failed to train us—or tell us, or communicate to us. If you take on some of the burden yourself, rather than just putting us down by stating how we should change, we'll be less defensive. We'll listen more closely. And, in a spirit of joint effort, we'll be more likely to try to fulfill our end of the bargain; we'll be more likely to improve.

When we really make a mistake, cool off. Don't attack us then. If you do, you'll say things you really don't mean, or things you really mean but shouldn't say. Either way, you'll tear the fabric of our boss/subordinate relationship. It might be a long time, if ever, before the damage from the angry attacks mends. You might want to change our behavior, but we doubt that you intend to endanger our relationship with you.

Here's another suggestion for performance reviews: start by asking *us* to evaluate our own performance. Then, where you agree with us, you can acknowledge the agreement (rather than attack us) and ask us what we can do to improve. Our acknowledgement of our own failings gets you halfway to solving the problem. Moreover, we'll walk out feeling as though you're helping, not attacking.

Probably the best test is to ask us at the end of the review session what we'll do differently. Don't accept just a list of things we *won't* do. Don't accept, "I'll work harder." Working harder, but still wrong, means we'll make more mistakes, not fewer. Make us tell you clearly what we'll do, what new behaviors we'll demonstrate. Then you'll know where each of us stands. And you'll sense whether we know what to do. If we don't, coach us, train us, develop us.

Dear Boss:

Re: **Poor Performance**

One major demand on your time is dealing with our poor performance. Generally, as soon as you point out some flaw in the way we're behaving, you act as if we should adjust our behavior immediately and completely. But sometimes your requests are unreasonable because our behavior is reasonable, even though you might not like it. Take personal appearance, for example. We accept the need for office decorum, but we should be able to wear our hair and clothes the way we want. If we use too much makeup, cologne, or jewelry for your taste, who has the problem, you or us?

At other times your request is reasonable, but we have trouble changing our behavior. You might think we're just lazy or reluctant to change, but sometimes change is difficult. If it were always easy, many psychologists would be unemployed!

Let us share with you a few of our observations about poor performance. Maybe they'll help you deal better with behavior you find unacceptable.

But first, what is unacceptable behavior? We all have our own definitions. For our purposes we'd like to focus on undesired behaviors that we repeat. We all make mistakes. If we hear about our mistakes, we try hard to avoid them. But when a mistake reoccurs, it signifies a problem in education, motivation, or behavior.

When people simply don't know what to do (even though they might feel, in their own minds, that they *should* know), you can simply educate them through training.

Usually this lack of know-how explains their unacceptable behavior. Don't assume they know how to do the task; even if they should know how to do it, they might not.

If people do know how to do a job—probably best proved by their past success—but still perform poorly, the problem might be motivation. We've already been sharing with you all we know about motivation. If you follow our advice, and performance still doesn't improve, then you might be dealing with a behavioral problem that goes beyond just simple motivation issues.

We don't think you should try to become a psychologist, but here are some ideas you might find useful. First, remember that poor performance is very probably a symptom of some other problem: financial, family, or health problems are typical. Trying to correct just the symptom, poor behavior, neither solves the problem nor removes the symptom for very long.

If you find out from employees or their co-workers that the root cause is a personal problem, you can do very little. Probably your best course of action is to help reduce, not increase, their stress. Become their ally. Acknowledge the problem and validate the stress they're feeling. Let them feel as though you're in their corner. We're not just making a plea for sympathy. On the contrary, this course of action is one of the best you can take to control poor behavior. By being an ally, by showing that you understand, you toss out a life preserver into our personal sea of emotional turbulence. To hold onto that life preserver, we'll try not to let you down, so we now have a new and selfish motive to meet your expectations.

Be sure to make it our responsibility to come to you if we can't make it, if we can't solve the problems surrounding our poor behavior. If that occurs, you can suggest whatever other options you find acceptable. And since we now see you as an ally, we'll be more likely to listen to your suggestions that we get counseling, use our vacation or sick leave, take a transfer (or even a termination), resign, or whatever else is appropriate.

This approach comes with no guarantees. but if a personal crisis interferes with someone's behavior, what other effective options do you have? Does adding more pressure with threats of discipline really make any sense? How will the rest of us view you as a boss when we learn that you're disciplining someone who's already going through a major crisis? Besides, if you stick by us during our personal crises, you'll earn our deep loyalty and commitment for a long time after the crises pass.

If you feel as though you're making very little progress toward finding the causes of someone's poor performance, try dealing with its consequences instead. Don't tell the employee, "Change or the consequences will be severe." Sure, that might work, but it really doesn't promote long-term motivation and good performance. In fact, some people might react in a passive-aggressive manner, to get even with you for your threat. Instead, discuss the consequences Socratically. Ask poor performers what they think the effects of their continued behavior will be. Get them to focus on the consequences of their behavior, free of threats. Discuss with them what they would do if they were managers. Don't judge, don't decide, and don't threaten. Just ask them about the consequences of their behavior and ask what they would do if they held your job as boss.

Show them that they have choices. Let them feel as though they can make decisions to behave differently, and remind them that you're there as an ally to help them through the transition.

Dear Boss:

Re: **Showing Anger**

We all lose our tempers from time to time. Perhaps it's only human. But when you lose your temper and get angry at us, you rip the fabric of our relationship. In time the anger and hurt subside, but it takes a long time to reweave the threads that bond us—boss and subordinates —into a cohesive team.

During the time when these connecting threads are being rewoven, we remain extraordinarily sensitive to further attacks. We've seen your anger once; we expect to see it again. And because we're expecting anger, we misinterpret your other actions as anger, even when no anger is intended. We're apt, for example, to misinterpret facetiousness or poking fun as toned-down attacks motivated by anger. Intentionally or not, you cut more threads.

Hard though it might be to accept, we each grow angry as a matter of choice; no one makes us that way. We *choose* to be upset. And when we're really angry—beyond what the situation calls for—it often means we're angry for other reasons. Too often frustrations we feel in other parts of our life, such as marital problems, carry over into our work. Then, something triggers the anger. Our reaction is exaggerated, propelled by our bottled-up feelings. We threaten, shout, even scream, further tearing the threads that unite us as a work team. Remember, as the great psychologist Alfred Adler observed, "We must interpret a bad temper as a sign of inferiority."

As Daniel Webster noted, anger is not an argument. In fact the only thing anger really proves is that whoever made you angry has defeated your self-control. If you get mad at us, we often get angry back—after all, we're no better than you are. We'd *all* be better off if we remembered the German saying, "The only answer to anger is silence." But once we let anger into our relationship, we sometimes find it difficult to remember that *anger* and *danger* are separated by only one letter.

Some thinkers believe that anger is merely a reflection of our fears. When we're brought into touch with our fears, we vent our stored-up emotions. And when we vent them as anger, our next step is to direct that anger outward. If we can't direct it at someone, we might redirect it at something, perhaps by slamming a door or pounding a fist.

The initial trigger for your anger might be something as simple as telling us to do something for a second or third time. Anger is a common reaction in such situations, but why? Are you angry because you're frustrated with us? Or are you more fearful of losing control, of not getting the task done, of looking foolish to us or to your boss? If you fear losing control, anger can swell up inside you until it's triggered by even a minor event. Then you vent. After you show your anger, it subsides...until the next time.

When the next time occurs, try two new courses of action. First, consider why you're so angry. No, not just the immediate cause—the mistake, the late report, the increase in scrap, or whatever. Look for the underlying issue. Is it a fear of looking foolish to your boss? Your peers? Yourself? Why are you so upset? Would you be that upset if an employee in another department did the same thing? Or if your employees made the same mistakes in their personal lives? Consider the specific incident not as the cause of your anger, but rather as the catalyst that triggers your real fears. What are those fears?

Now comes the tough part. Once you identify the fear, get rid of it by expressing it. Tell the person at whom you would normally be angry why you're upset. Be sure to use *I* statements: "I'm upset when a report is late because I feel disrespected. That feeling of disrespect, combined with the late report, make me feel out of control, even foolish. So I get angry. Rather than get angry at you, I want you to know why late reports evoke such a strong reaction."

Feeling lucky to get out of your office alive, even fully lobotomized morons will reflect on how you handled the situation. If you had attacked them with an outburst of anger, you would have triggered their defenses, probably strings of excuses and blame laid on some other culprit. They would have stopped listening. They would have seen you as needlessly (or overly) angry and *out of control.*

But by explaining in the first person, using *I* statements, you avoided attacking the second person with *you* accusations. You explained *why* late reports are unacceptable. When you speak calmly in the first person, employees have fewer reasons to become defensive and block out your communications. They continue listening. They see you as in control of yourself.

The key to this process is controlling your anger. Sometimes it's very tough not to explode. Even the best leaders lose their concentration and vent their fears by getting angry at someone. To reduce such unpleasant episodes to a minimum requires another step: getting in touch with the inner fear that provokes your anger. Once you find that fear, expressing it drains some of its energy. And if you reveal your fear—whether it's feeling out of control, disrespected, or whatever—then your concern over the late report seems reasonable on a personal, human-to-human level. Your employees see you as rational, in control of your emotions, and open. And since you're being open without attacking, you have each culprit's attention and respect. You're communicating on a very basic level, one the report writers can't easily forget or rationalize away.

Ultimately, we must realize what Viktor Frankl discovered in the concentration camps of World War II: we are each responsible for our own feelings and attitudes. If you let a late report cause you to explode, if you elect to blame others, then you're letting someone else shape your attitudes. If, instead, you express your concerns as *I* statements, then you remain in control, in charge of your attitudes.

Dear Boss:

Re: **Effective Discipline**

What's your goal when you discipline us? We think it should be to change the results of our behavior. The purpose of discipline isn't to punish or demonstrate your superiority. No, discipline should be corrective. If we persist in our behavior, then the discipline should become progressively stiffer, with stiffer penalties. But, it should still remain corrective, not punitive.

Please keep these three simple thoughts in mind the next time you discipline someone.

1. Just because an approach works for you doesn't mean it works for everyone.
2. Be sure to criticize the performance, not the performer.
3. Remember that the aim of criticism is to have us feel as though we've been helped, not belittled.

For discipline to be effective and corrective, you should use the "Hot Stove" and "Sandwich" rules. First, think about how a hot stove administers discipline when we touch it. Its discipline is fast and consistent. The quick response helps us associate our action (touching the stove) with the discipline (being burned). And the stove disciplines every offender equally, making it consistent. It's also impersonal; it doesn't attack our egos by questioning our intelligence or parentage. And, since we're all adults and know that we shouldn't touch a hot stove, its discipline is based on a clear warning. The hot stove metes out discipline quickly, consistently, and impersonally after giving us a warning. Just following the Hot Stove Rule would be a big improvement for many bosses we've had. All we need to add is, do it in private.

Unlike hot stoves, bosses should discipline in private—for everyone's benefit. If the discipline is public, we're likely to be more concerned about what our peers think than about learning from our mistakes. Not only does our embarrassment block communications, it also can lead to some form of retaliation ("I'll fix that boss!"). Perhaps that "fix" will never come. But what if it does, at the expense of productivity (sabotage or a slowdown, for example)? Or what if the temptation to embarrass the boss leads to a verbal confrontation? Disciplining in private cuts down on retaliation.

The Sandwich Rule has to do with how you implement the Hot Stove Rule. Again, keep in mind that discipline is not supposed to be punitive, it's supposed to change our behavior. Too often, however, bosses go straight at the problem, with no buffer, using an approach like dumping a load of bricks on the wrongdoer. Sandwiching the Hot Stove part between two pieces of reassurance makes the discipline more effective.

Suppose, for example, that the discipline problem is tardiness. Usually you confront the wrongdoer about the problem and get a load of reasons and excuses in return. Instead, try using the Sandwich approach by placing the Hot Stove between two positive comments about the employee:

> You're a good worker. You produce quality
> parts for us. Some of our customers even ask for
> you by name, they're so pleased by the work you

do. And I appreciate your concern for quality and customer satisfaction. My problem is your tardiness. Not only is it disruptive, it's also unfair for me to expect others to be on time and let you waltz in here late. I need your help to end your tardiness.

You are a good employee! You've got a good attitude and a great attendance record. Why, I can't remember the last time you missed a day. All around I'm glad you work here. Keep up your good work and I'm sure everything will smooth out.

When you start the discipline process by describing our wrongdoing, our defense mechanisms go up and communications break down. Even in private the discipline feels like an attack: we're being accused of doing something wrong. Our normal reaction is to think of reasons, rationalizations, and excuses. We stop listening. We're too busy trying to defend ourselves verbally and psychologically. But when you start the process by buffering the bad news with recognition of our good points, we become more receptive to your communication. We listen more carefully. Then, when we hear the criticism inherent in the discipline, it seems more balanced. If you can recognize our strengths, then we can accept that maybe our actions were wrong. If, on the other hand, you discipline us without buffering the bad news by acknowledging our good points, both you and the criticism seem unfair.

CHAPTER 8
WORKING AS A TEAM

Dear Boss:

Re: Allies

Most bosses want to appear as though they are in charge of everything. But your need to appear self-sufficient may cut you off from people who could be allies. So treat us as though we're your allies, not your subordinates. Some of us are just waiting for you to enlist our support.

Besides, no matter whether you're dealing with subordinates or peers, sooner or later you'll need help. You're much more likely to receive it from people who feel like allies than from those who feel subordinated or alienated. You might never need a favor from some people. But if you have a large number of allies throughout the organization, you'll have a good internal public relations network—a network of people who think highly of you. That can't hurt your career! And when you need a favor—an extra effort to reach a tough goal, for example—your allies will come to your aid. Even those who aren't yet your allies might pitch in because they too hope to create an alliance. Besides, the dignity and respect you afford an ally creates an adult-to-adult relationship, rather than a childlike dependency.

Dear Boss:

Re: Resistance to Change

Have you ever encountered resistance to change? Of course you have! All bosses do from time to time. If you'd like to reduce our resistance to change, you can do it by remembering that people don't resist their own ideas.

Use our ideas to solve problems, and we'll attack the problems with vigor. We'll feel responsible for finding solutions that we can make work. But how do you tap that wellspring of motivation? You do it by letting us define problems and discover solutions. By getting us involved in the decision-making process.

Your first attempts at participative decision making will probably encounter resistance. We'll be suspicious: does the boss *really* want our ideas or is this just some ploy to get us to "discover" what the boss has already decided? If you persist in inviting our input, we'll test you by proposing a solution to some problem *we* have. The problem and solution might be of little interest to you; you might even find that the solution offers few benefits to either you or the organization. But we will persist in our recommendation. If you reject our idea without solid, well-explained reasons, we'll conclude that you weren't really serious about involving us in decision making.

If you use one of our ideas, even if it's not the "best" solution, you'll earn our support. Our resistance will fade because we don't resist our own ideas. If, on the other hand, you hold out for your own alternative, convinced that it's best, you'll win, we'll use your idea. But you'll also lose because you won't get our wholehearted commitment.

    We want to feel that we are a part of what's happening around here. When you involve us and use our ideas, we will feel motivated rather than resistant.

Dear Boss:

Re: **Making Decisions**

You're not paid to make decisions; you're paid to get decisions made. That might sound picky, but the distinction drives to the heart of effective decision making, good leadership, and motivation. When you make a decision by yourself, you deny us a chance to be creative.

Our ideas are not threats. You don't need to demonstrate your power by disregarding them; using them is not a sign of weakness in you. Nor are our thoughts attacks on your self-worth. If you're truly concerned about how you really appear to us, then seek out and use our ideas. Use them even if yours are better. You'll look more confident and get fresh insights. And your decisions will be better and more widely supported.

Watch how this process works:

Step 1. Recognizing and Formulating Problems or Opportunities. You're the one who usually decides whether a problem or an opportunity exists. You recognize it. You define it. The result? It's *your* problem. Since we seldom get to define the problem, we feel no sense of ownership for it.

Step 2. Generating Alternatives. Next, you generate some possible solutions. They're *your* solutions, not ours. Again, we feel no ownership.

Step 3. Selecting an Alternative. Now you pick one alternative. At that point you become committed to your solution. You own it. You read our indifference to your solution, our apathy, as resistance. You see anyone who objects as resisting your idea, resisting what you want.

Step 4. Implementation. At this stage you start to implement your solution. Since we had no involvement in developing this solution, we don't understand why it's the best one, even though it's advantages might be obvious to you. Since it's your problem, your alternative, and your solution, we feel no ownership in, and therefore no commitment to, your decision.

Step 5. Control and Follow-up. Since we lack strong commitment to your decision, you need to apply more controls so the results match your expectations. You end up spending a lot more time following up because we're implementing your decision, not ours.

If, on the other hand, you involve us in the decision-making process, we get the enjoyment of seeing our ideas work. And when we use our ideas, you get our commitment and motivation instead of resistance to your decision.

Most of the other managers for whom we have worked found it difficult to involve employees in decision making. Some felt it would be abdicating their own responsibilities. In their own careers they'd only worked for managers who made all the decisions themselves, so they thought participation was wrong. Worse still, many feared they would look indecisive—or even weak or incapable—if they invited employee involvement.[6] Many bosses believed their own ideas were somehow better than those of their employees, so why use second-best ideas? All these bosses were too unskilled and uncertain to break away from the traditional I'm-the-boss-and-I-make-the-decisions mentality.

Some bosses argue that involvement is too time consuming. But decisiveness is what counts! Involving employees does slow down the first two steps toward taking action, formulating the problem and generating alternatives (Figure 1). But notice what happens in the implementation stage. Implementation goes quickly because there's little resistance to change. Likewise, you need less follow-up because employees who are involved and using their own ideas need little control. Are both styles of decision making equally fast, as the figure suggests? We don't know. We do know, however, that our morale, motivation, pride, commitment, satisfaction, and understanding are higher when we participate.

Still unconvinced? Ask yourself which style of decision making you would want your own boss to use? Do you think our answer is any different? We want the same things you want, including a chance to use our skills while earning feelings of achievement, accomplishment, and recognition. Which approach to decision making should you use day after day?

Figure 1

The Time Involved in Decision Making: Authoritative vs. Participative

	Time Involved	
	Authoritative Old Style	Participative New Style
1. Recognizing and Formulating Problems and Opportunities	1	1
	2	
2. Generating Alternatives	3	2
3. Selecting an Alternative	4	3
4. Implementation		4
5. Control and Follow-up	5	5

Dear Boss:

Re: The Purpose of Planning

As a follow-up to the memo on "Making Decisions," consider how participative decision making affects the planning process around here.

Most bosses think that the purpose of planning is to create a picture of the future. And, certainly, having such a blueprint is one important outcome of the planning process. But, the other outcome of planning might be even more important.

Done correctly, the planning process helps build consensus through participation. This consensus creates a sense of shared ownership in the plan, which leads in turn to greater commitment. Interestingly, it's this commitment that helps assure the plan's success. So you see, the planning process might be even more important than the resulting plan!

Dear Boss:

Re: The Glory Multiplier

Everyone likes to share in the glory. We all like to get credit. But, "Where's the glory?" might be a fair question around here. When we do something noteworthy, we should get the glory. But too often it seems as though the glory goes to you without any credit to us. Later, we hear an announcement that the organization will be using "your idea." We feel as though you stole both our idea and our glory. And when you do that, you miss the advantages of the Glory Multiplier.

You can't subtract or divide glory, you can only add or multiply it. What happens if one of us gives you a good idea, and you convince your boss that it's yours? You get the credit for it; you look good in your boss's eyes. But what would happen if you told your boss it came from one of us? You'd still get credit for it. And you'd also get credit for stimulating creativity among your employees. Then, when the company announced the idea, the originator would get some credit—and you might even get credit for not stealing it. Other employees would also see that you give credit by sharing the glory. The result? Instead of just getting credit from your boss, you'd also get credit from the idea's originator and the rest of us as well. You would create an atmosphere where we would be more willing to be creative. We'd become more willing to make you look good!

When you share glory, you multiply it; you even multiply your own share. And when you share it with us, imagine what happens to our attitude, morale, motivation, and pride.

Dear Boss:

Re: **Support Follows Understanding**

Too often you try to win our support for something we don't understand. To honestly support your ideas, we need to understand them and the reasons behind them. If you don't explain your reasons—or worse, if you intentionally hold back your key reasons—can you really expect us to support your ideas?

Understanding—*our* understanding—must precede our support. As William R. Laidig of Great Northern Nekoosa observed shortly after he became Chief Executive Officer, "I learned that if I couldn't get the crew I wanted to apply an idea to appreciate and understand it, then it was a lousy idea whether I thought so or not."[7]

People cannot thoroughly support what they don't understand. The more you can communicate with us about goals, constraints, and your needs, the better we will understand, and the better we can support you.

Dear Boss:

Re: **Power Bases**

You're the boss because the organization has given you the authority to direct us. It has also given you responsibility for making decisions and taking action. But having authority and using it effectively are two very different things.

When you give an order based on your authority, we usually obey it because the consequences of disobeying it might be severe. However, when we follow your orders just because you're the boss, we don't follow them very enthusiastically. Most of us don't like to be told what to do. When someone orders us to do something, we give our commitment grudgingly, at best.

If you can't win our wholehearted support with a direct order, how can you gain our enthusiasm? Most textbooks and management thinkers agree that your job as a manager is getting things done through people, but that's incorrect. You don't get it done *through* us. A better definition of management is getting things done *with* people. If, as this definition implies, you can make us feel as if we're part of the process of getting things done around here, we're more likely to be supportive. By involving us in the decision-making process, you recognize our worth and our potential contribution. The result is team spirit. All you have to do is ask for—and use—our ideas.

Besides formal authority and inviting participation, you have several other bases of power open to you. One is knowledge. If we perceive you as more knowledgeable than we are, we're much more likely to follow your lead.

You might remember that when Spiro Agnew became President Nixon's first vice president, he was the former governor of Maryland, and had neither a nationwide political constituency nor experience in the U.S. Senate. In fact the press greeted his nomination on the Republican ticket with such headlines as, "Spiro Who?" Yet shortly after the 1968 election, he found himself presiding over the U.S. Senate, his only constitutionally prescribed duty besides succeeding the president. Imagine him (or anyone) trying to exert "formal authority" over one hundred independent-minded senators! Instead, he relied on his recently acquired expertise about the rules, procedures, and traditions of the U.S. Senate. No, senators didn't suddenly proxy their votes with him. But despite his relative obscurity the previous summer, he earned the respect of many senators. Why? Because he relied not on his formal authority, but on the power of expertise.

Had Agnew been a highly revered national politician or religious leader, senators might have deferred to him out of respect. Had he been charismatic, his personal magnetism might have carried the day. Revered and charismatic people can use these personal characteristics as bases of power. But people like these are rare, so we seldom have them as bosses.

The only remaining bases of power are reward and punishment. Both form an integral part of formal authority. But as Captain Bligh found out after the mutiny on the *Bounty*, "Whom they fear, they hate." Punishment doesn't foster loyal, dedicated teamwork. And rewards often prove nearly as ineffective because so few are available to most bosses.

So when we look at you we see rewards and personal traits like charisma as possible but somewhat impractical bases from which to draw your power. Formal authority and coercion work, but they exact too high a price in morale and loyalty.

What's left? For all practical purposes, not much. You can do your best to become an expert so we'll defer to your expertise. And you can expand and strengthen your authority by sharing it with us through more participative decision making. If you think the latter is abdicating your role as boss, remember that you're not paid to make decisions, you're paid to get them made. You're paid to get them made efficiently and effectively, while engendering the support of your subordinates, us. And ultimately there are only two types of power in an organization: the formal, from-the-top-down authority granted to all bosses by their superiors; and the informal, from-the-bottom-up authority that grows from the employees' acceptance of their boss. You can earn our acceptance, and therefore avoid using your formal authority, by sharing your authority with us, and by letting us have a larger say in what happens.

Dear Boss:

Re: Organization Charts and Other Accoutrements

We all know that organization charts are, at best, approximations of reality. Many informal relationships don't even show up on them. And formal relationships change so fast the charts are often outdated even before they're finalized and printed.

But what really bothers us about organization charts is what they imply. By showing the hierarchical structure, they imply that employees work for their boss, that we work for you. And in many conventional ways, we do. But that attitude—employees working *for* their bosses—causes many of the problems that occur between managers and workers. Managers soon feel, then act, superior. The power of authority becomes a wedge between them and the workers. Soon an invisible—but nevertheless real—wall goes up, a wall built of arrogance and false pride.

The wall is then reinforced with other accoutrements: nicer desks, carpets, expense accounts, company cars, and the like. These accoutrements further widen the gap separating our organization into two classes. The result is resentment and lower productivity.

Sure, rank has its privileges. Sure, there should be some incentive for moving up through the traditional hierarchy. But must those incentives widen the gap between us and management?

We'd like to suggest redoing the organization chart with employees at the top and the bosses underneath. That format reminds everyone that the role of the boss is to support and assist us in doing our job. We also think that a more egalitarian approach to the accoutrements of organizational life can break down some of the symbols of status. Do we really need those symbols to make the organization effective? We are not suggesting a totally egalitarian view. We just hope that you can play down those symbols of organizational power.

Dear Boss:

Re: **Personality Types**

If you really want to be an effective manager, you might consider how differences in our personalities shape how we behave. Psychiatrists suggest that four pairs of variables lie at the heart of personality. Each pair of terms anchors two ends of a continuum:

- Extroversion or Introversion
- Sensing or Intuition
- Thinking or Feeling
- Judging or Perceiving

Extroverts relate well to people. They're very likely to tell you their opinions. In fact, if you don't know how an extrovert feels, you haven't been listening! Introverts, however, are less likely to volunteer their feelings. They're more likely to keep them private, hiding them from all but the most confidential of their allies.

Understanding this difference can be crucial to your success as a boss. For those of us who are introverts, you'll have to work more diligently to get us to reveal our feelings, opinions, and ideas. When you ask for suggestions or feedback, the extroverts among us are more likely to speak up. So the introverts, unless you encourage them, might make a far smaller contribution. But neither intelligence nor creativity favors extroverts; introverts are just as likely to have good ideas. You'll need to work harder, perhaps even mount a concerted effort, to solicit their input. Getting their opinions is especially crucial when your decisions will affect them personally. Just because they don't complain doesn't mean they don't have any complaints! You must actively and sincerely seek their suggestions and ideas, especially if you're an extrovert who assumes others will volunteer their feelings.

Another pair of personality variables is sensing vs. intuition. Sensing types base decisions on data they get through their senses. They're the people who sometimes ask the embarrassing (but often needed) question, "What do the data show?" They also tend to be better at details than their intuitive counterparts (many of our accountants and engineers, for example, are sensing types). Intuitive types are less grounded by the reality of data. They focus more on the broad possibilities that underlie the data—if they even look at the data at all. This ability to see other possibilities often puts them in creative jobs, positions that rely less on analysis than on imagination (advertising and sales are common strongholds for intuitive types).

No matter which type you are—intuitive or sensing—you might find opposite personality types upsetting. If you're a sensing type, you expect the people around you to generate and rely on objective data. You might feel as though intuitive types, especially if undisciplined, usually find approximations close enough. To your eye they simply don't exhibit enough attention to detail. If you're an intuitive leader, on the other hand, sensing types might bore you with their reams of data, numbers, and endless explanations.

As a leader you need to have both personality types around you: sensing types to provide details and accuracy, and intuitive types to furnish the creativity to see underlying possibilities.

The third pair of variables is thinking vs. feeling. These descriptions provide merely a clue to people's first responses. A thinker relies on basic principles (right and wrong, for example) and uses logic to arrive at a well-thought-out decision. Then, almost as an afterthought, the thinker considers how other people might feel about the decision. Feelers, on the other hand, are just the opposite: they first consider people's feelings about the situation before thinking it through and applying rules, policies, or principles. These responses are first reactions—thinkers think first, while feelers feel first. But thinkers also feel, just as feelers also think.

Thinkers must be careful to weigh the emotional reactions to their decision or they'll look too unfeeling and analytical to feeling types. And feelers need to make sure they're being logical and systematic, not just sympathetic, or they'll look soft, wishy-washy, or unbusinesslike to thinkers.

The final pair of personality variables are judging and perceiving. Judging types find it easier to make decisions promptly. Based on the information avaliable, they can make a decision and move on. Perceiving types often see less urgency in making decisions, preferring to gain additional information before making the final decision. What may appear to be procrastination to a judging type may be the perceiving type's on-going willingness to consider additional information.

With each pair of variables, neither one type nor the other is better, they're just different. As a boss you need *all* the different personality types to assure balanced support that includes thinking and feeling, sensing and intuition, and judging and perceiving.

The trap bosses face is the tendency to clone themselves. But hiring only people who think as you do might lead to having no feeling types among your staff. And if you can't tolerate intuitive types because of their limited attention to details—or sensing types because of their overemphasis on details—you'll further homogenize your staff. Internal dissention might decline, but your staff might also acquire a terminal case of myopia that inevitably will distort your judgment, too.

The key is *balance.* Having a diverse staff might lead to more internal dissention because you'll get more diverse opinions, especially if you actively seek the opinions of introverts. But it will also provide a rich variety of viewpoints.

So please remember that each of us has a unique personality that offers you both strengths and weaknesses. As you come to learn more about each of us, you'll be able to use us better in situations that draw on our strengths and minimize our weaknesses. Until then, you'll make the mistake of asking sensing types to do creative work and intuitive types to address details, with disappointing results. When disappointment surfaces, see if you can spot the personality differences involved. Once you learn to recognize, accept, and even appreciate our differences, you'll be a far more effective leader.

Dear Boss:

Re: **The Informal Organization**

You're the formal leader of our department. With that position you gained the formal authority bestowed on you by your boss. But the formal part of the organization is only one side.

The informal side influences the organization's actions, too. Perhaps you're aware of this informal side—perhaps you even pay homage to it—but we think you'd be more effective if you actively considered the informal organization before you make a crucial decision.

The informal organization is the glue that cements this collection of people into a unit. It's through friendships and our peer group that we meet our personal needs. Without that emotional support, we'd find this organization a sterile place to work. Without the informal network of friendships and favors, much of the work around here wouldn't get done. So you need the informal group as much as we do, both to satisfy your personal needs and to facilitate getting the work done.

Of particular importance are informal leaders. No one appoints them to be the spokespersons for our group; they simply emerge. They emerge as leaders because they understand how the group works and what it needs. Often they're better than we are at expressing the group's thoughts and needs. Usually they're long-tenured members of the group who are more outspoken than most of us.

If you ignore these informal leaders, you do so at your own peril. They can offer you a quick reading of the group's feelings. But if you ignore them, they might exhibit their leadership roles by rebelling against your wishes, like ill-mannered children who defy the authority of an adult telling them to behave. Or worse, they might suggest that we do *exactly* what we've been told, without using our common sense.

On a more subtle level, informal leaders are the group's reference point. Many times your requests strike indifferent ears and undecided minds. Our informal leaders can quickly and permanently decide our attitudes—for better or worse—with a few utterances or even a look. If the leaders dislike the vacation schedule, their opinion can sour us all on it. And dissension leads to declining morale. A constructive word from our informal leaders, on the other hand, might well turn our indifferent ears and undecided minds in the other direction.

Identify and then consult with these cornerstones of groupthink. Ignoring them, issuing orders that don't acknowledge these leaders' roles as cohesive forces in the group, is risking challenges to your leadership in often subtle but damning ways.

Recognize the informal leaders. Work with them; solicit their opinions. If you do, you will gain more support from the informal organization and find our opinion leaders to be on your side.

CHAPTER 9
STAFFING ISSUES

Dear Boss:

Re: **Empire Building**

We know that salaries reflect responsibilities. We also understand that one measure of your responsibility is the number of people you supervise. The people who determine salaries relied for a long time on numbers of people supervised. So we begin this memo by acknowledging that it's to your wallet's advantage to build an empire even at the expense of overstaffing.

As we add more people, however, our department's effectiveness doesn't necessarily grow in proportion. Each additional person is a recruiting, hiring, training, and maintenance expense. And we don't pay all these expenses with money; some of them cost us time as well. We have to forgo our own work to recruit, hire, and train each new addition. You must devote your time to coaching, evaluating, and counseling them. And you must devote more and more of your time to holding together the social fabric of our department. Soon you'll need help supervising all these new additions, so you'll have to hire still more people.

As your empire continues to grow, new layers of management will come between you and us. Do you think we have communication problems now? Wait until you have another layer of supervisors between you and us! Communication will grow even worse. In time, our department's effectiveness will suffer. Costs will be up and performance down.

Don't misunderstand us; we know that as we grow, you'll need to hire more people. But do it sparingly. First, be sure those of us already here have all the tools and resources we need to do our best. Sure, it might be easier to get a $20,000-a-year employee than a $15,000 computer and peripherals. And we know that another body increases the size and, therefore, the prestige of your empire. Clearly, the temptation to add more people is strong. But resist that temptation! If our department remains lean and mean, we'll have better job security, and you'll have fewer employee-relations issues to distract you. Besides, a reputation as a cost-effective manager who works people hard but takes care of them will help your career more than running a bloated, overstaffed department will.

A car gets better mileage at fifty miles an hour rather than ninety because it expends less energy overcoming internal friction. And you'll get better mileage out of your department if you give us the tools and security that don't exist in an overstaffed empire.

Dear Boss:

Re: **High Turnover**

We're your most important assets. We handle the department's customers and make everything work around here. If you recognized us as the important assets we are, you'd be a lot more concerned when someone leaves. But losing people doesn't trouble you. And that makes us feel as though people really don't matter to you. Imagine if every department employee stole a desk top computer when they left! You'd notice that loss of hard assets right away. Well, the cost of recruiting, selecting, and training a new employee costs more than a new personal computer! Yet these walking assets keep walking right out the door and you show little concern.

Consider what happens when we have turnover. New employees report to work and you chat with them for a few minutes. Then you ask us to show the new workers around. We do. And we consider being asked to orient new employees a compliment. But while we devote our time to bringing them up to speed, we fall behind in our own work.

Normally, this extra effort would be just part of the job. Turnover is so high, however, that several problems arise. First, we feel as though our efforts are largely futile, since high turnover is likely to continue—the employee we train today will probably leave tomorrow. Second, we become overworked. We experienced employees work harder to compensate for the inexperienced ones. The additional workload means we make more mistakes, for which we get criticism. So we work harder but get more criticism.

Even the added criticism might be tolerable if you also gave us more recognition for the added burdens we shoulder. Since most people don't quit until they find a better-paying job, high turnover causes us to rethink our pay, our commitment to you, and our jobs themselves.

Perhaps if the accountants made you budget and control your recruiting, selection, and training costs, you'd pay more attention to turnover. But these figures don't show up in either our budget or our profit-and-loss statement. Yet during their weeks—even months—of training, new employees' performance is below that of the average trained employee. The rest of us suffer by trying to keep up the unit's level of performance. Let us know you appreciate our efforts and are concerned when people leave.

Remember, turnover is not a problem, it's a symptom! It reflects the quality of treatment we receive. Sure, some people quit to retire, raise families, or move away from the area. But we're not talking about that type of turnover. We're concerned with the turnover that results when people quit to go to another organization.

Sometimes they're new employees who find out our work just isn't for them; after they've started, they realize they'd rather do something else. Frankly, there's little you can do about turnover among new-hires who experience a conflict of expectations. You might try giving new-hires a realistic job preview, where they can see the work being done, visit the work area, and even talk with those of us who work there. Perhaps that would reduce turnover among new-hires. But what about the rest of us who have been here for a while but aren't locked in with pension benefits, extra-long vacations, or other benefit-based handcuffs?

If you agree that most turnover is a symptom of managerial treatment, and you really want to reduce the turnover, try two specific courses of action: exit interviews and attitude surveys.

Conduct exit interviews with departing employees to find out why they're leaving and what would have encouraged them to stay. Don't be duped by the standard answer to, "Why are you leaving?" Virtually everyone answers, "Higher pay!" The real question is not, "Why are you leaving?," but "Why did you go looking for another job?" Most people aren't going to leave for lower pay. Instead, once they've decided to leave, they'll stay until they find another job with higher pay. When they're asked, "Why did you leave?" their answer about higher pay is simple and truthful, but not very insightful.

If you really want the exit interview to be meaningful, conduct it yourself; don't delegate it and get just an obscure summary. Look departing employees in the eye and ask them why they decided to look for another job. Then ask them, "What could we have done differently that would have caused you to stay?" Finally, ask straight out, "What changes need to be made around here?" You might not like the answers you hear, but if you follow up on them with corrective action, turnover will drop.

Another great tool to find out the problems underlying high turnover is the attitude survey. As the earlier memo on attitude surveys pointed out, it's not just people's attitudes that are important, it's their perceptions about whether the organization is becoming a better or worse place to work. Those perceptions are vitally important. Seeing you conduct and follow up on exit interviews will lead employees to believe our organization is becoming a better place to work.

After all, if people are known by the company they keep, then a company is known by the people it keeps!

Dear Boss:

Re: **Selection**

Pick people who are better than either you or us. If we keep selecting people who are less qualified than we are, we'll just pull down the average quality of our work force. What Carl Icahn, the corporate financier, observed about corporate boardrooms probably applies to us as well: "What goes on in the boardroom is a travesty. And the chairman doesn't want someone under him who is a threat. So he picks someone a little less capable. It's like an anti-Darwinian theory—the survival of the unfittest. And, it's getting worse."[8]

Perhaps no other action is more important than the hiring decision. Why not ask us to interview candidates, too? We'll feel more committed to helping those newcomers we helped to choose. The more input you get about a hiring decision, the better that decision will be. The better job we do of selection, the better organization we'll have.

Dear Boss:

Re: Experienced People

When we go to hire a new person around here, we place too much emphasis on applicants' experience. Sure, experience is helpful, even necessary. But what do we really get when we seek someone with "five years of experience"? Sometimes we get a person with a wealth of background upon which they can draw. But often we get someone who merely has had one year of experience repeated five times.

As Oscar Wilde observed, "Experience is the name everyone gives to their mistakes." When we hire experienced people, their experience doesn't necessarily mean they're better than anyone else. Instead, it might mean that they've simply made more mistakes. In the final analysis, Aldous Huxley probably said it best: "Experience is not what happens to you; it is what you do with what happens to you."

Dear Boss:

Re: Degrees

You know and we know that no one ever selects the "best" candidate for a job. Instead, what really happens is that you try to eliminate all the candidates but one. Usually it's much easier to say why a candidate is *not* qualified than to state why one applicant is better than another. So we make cuts from the potential pool of applicants by dropping those with some obviously disqualifying characteristic.

Probably no cut is more common, or more ill-advised, than dropping people because they lack a degree. We know it's a simple cut to make; it's objective and very common. But think through the implications. First of all, it might be illegal. Yes, illegal! Can you *prove* that the degree is a bona fide job requirement? Where are the scientific validation studies, supported by statistical evidence, that prove the degree is necessary? If you don't have conclusive proof, a "protected class" member (a minority member or a woman) could sue, charging you with discrimination. We don't think such a suit would benefit your career.

But we can suggest an even more compelling reason for disregarding degrees. Suppose you give people jobs that usually go to people with degrees. Sure, you might catch some flak from your bosses, who are likely to second-guess you, so you'd better have your arguments all lined up. But how do you think the new jobholders will react? First, their jobs probably will represent the promotion of a lifetime—maybe even the last one of a lifetime. Will such people be motivated? You bet! Their elation will translate into motivation. And yet elation doesn't last for long. What about their long-range attitudes and behavior? Well, these people are also likely to be motivated in the long run because their career options elsewhere are severely limited without the degree. They'll probably feel strong loyalty as a result.

Think about the reactions from other employees. They would see hiring or promotion decisions based on merit. Degree holders would realize that their competitors for promotions are more numerous than they thought. And other employees without degrees would realize that merit holds the key, that hard work—even in the absence of a degree—pays off.

Dear Boss:

Re: **Outplacement**

Sometimes people have to leave our organization. If they're being fired because of something they did wrong, or if they're leaving to seek other opportunities, they're on their own. But, if they're leaving involuntarily through no fault of their own, consider outplacement.

We spend a lot of money recruiting, selecting, hiring, orienting, training, and developing people. Certainly we can afford to help find employment for those who are forced to leave. To say that our company doesn't have an outplacement program merely sidesteps the issue. We could pool together and let people stay on the payroll, at least for a couple of weeks, while they look for other work. We could even let them use in-house typing, photocopying, and phone services for their job search.

We're not naive. We know that one of the major reasons people are laid off is to save money. So lay them off an extra week early and save even more money, so we can spend some time helping them make the transition. Besides, there's more to laying people off than just money.

What do you think happens to morale, motivation, performance, and costs when we see people tossed out—even if they were performing poorly? We view the organization as uncaring, so uncaring that it wouldn't help them during this difficult transition. Those of us remaining soon figure out that we'd better look out for ourselves, since the organization sure won't. That doesn't mean we're all going to rush out and form a union or quit. But our eager, loyal support will probably decline.

Dear Boss:

Re: Ex-employees

Consider what happens when people around here quit, especially to go to work for other employers. Shortly after they leave you begin character assassinations. Subtle criticisms give way to less subtle ones until you're blaming every problem since the Great Flood on the ex-employees.

Perhaps you feel betrayed. When people you once controlled walk out, your feelings of abandonment and lack of control might give way to a desire for revenge. And since the people have left, all you can do is assassinate their memory. But remember, some of us remain friends with those ex-employees, and your assassination attempts hurt us. They make us wonder, "What do you really think about me? Why are you so petty because someone sought a better career opportunity?"

Admittedly, your assassination attempts are less serious when people retire or leave for health reasons. But even then you make subtle digs. Do you need to make yourself feel important by putting other people down? Let's build up the memory of those who left so we can build morale and loyalty among those who remain behind. Let's create an attitude that says, "This place is the home of champions, past and present."

CHAPTER 10
THE BOTTOM LINE

Dear Boss:

Re: Cost Controls

We know costs must be controlled, but at what cost? We have controls on top of controls. In some cases the controls cost more than what they're trying to control! Why, just to get a dozen pencils we have to fill out a purchase requisition in triplicate, submit it, and wait a week or usually longer for them to arrive. Of course, that all assumes we filled out the purchase requisition correctly and didn't fail to specify alternate vendors. If we made an error (sin of sins!) we must redo the purchase request and wait another week. And this is just a trivial example (although a particularly annoying one).

A more fundamental problem concerns controls and initiative. We're so hung up on showing how we cut costs and save money that the documentation can cost *more* than the amount saved. Even worse, many of us are afraid to ask for money to innovate. The hurdles to get money for an innovation are so many and so high that otherwise-responsible people often say, "It's not worth the effort." Innovations sit in desk drawers and closed-off minds because of too much justification and documentation. This company is going to save itself right into obsolescence! Now, don't give us the lecture on Our Duty to Innovate. The time and emotional costs of innovation are just too high. It's much easier to sit back and wait for innovations to come from the top. As someone once observed, "We're too busy stepping over twenty-dollar bills so we can pick up the dimes."

What can we do? Perhaps you could create a task force to review the control procedures in our department. Then we could modify those we created and ask for modifications of those imposed upon us by accounting, purchasing, and others.

Dear Boss:

Re: **Costs vs. Investments**

Sometimes the labels we assign things lead to unintended consequences. Take the term *costs*. It's applied to virtually every outlay this organization makes, except for major investments. What's the distinction between a *cost* and an *investment*?

As we see it, an investment is something that provides an ongoing stream of benefits to the company, often for more than a year. Costs, on the other hand, are expenses for things we consume that provide no ongoing benefits, such as materials we buy. But aren't *all* the monies we spend actually investments that we hope will pay dividends to the organization? Aren't *expense accounts* really *investment accounts*, because the money we spend will presumably bring some benefit to the company? Aren't training expenses really investments? And aren't expenses on people really an investment in our human capital?

Rather than just changing the title of these accounts, let's start asking what the benefits are, not just the expenses. As we identify the benefits, we can better adjust our actual expenditures. The company gains, and we'll gain a better understanding of these costs.

Dear Boss:

Re: **Things vs. People**

Because of your training and probably your personality, you prefer to deal with objective numbers and tangible (or at least measurable) results.

Obviously not every technically trained manager fits this description. Some, in fact, broke out of their technical molds simply because they prefer people over things or numbers. However, all organizations harbor plenty of bosses who prefer the quantitative certainty of things to the qualitative uncertainty of people. Such leaders, when given the choice between spending limited resources on people or on things, often prefer the cold, hard facts of a capital-equipment purchase to the subjective guessing that surrounds decisions involving people. The result? A bias toward capital, not people.

What seems to be missing, boss, is the realization that capital is employed *by people*. It's people who make the equipment work well or poorly. To shortchange us is to shortchange the company's potential.

You want proof? We can't give you direct proof. But consider how many times we've bought a new machine and it didn't live up to our expectations. Was the machine defective, or were the people using it not doing their best? Don't misunderstand us; we realize capital is crucial to our success. New machines and equipment help us do a better job. All we're saying is that you should weigh very carefully how money is spent when it comes to capital versus people. And when you decide to spend it on capital, weigh carefully the roles of the people the decision will affect.

Suppose, for example, you decide to buy a new photocopier. You might make that decision solely on the basis of technical specifications—costs, number of copies per minute, and the like. But if those of us who use it, keep it in toner, unjam it, and make it perform have no say in the decision, how supportive are we likely to be? Will we be pleased or annoyed when it arrives? Will we make the extra little effort to load the paper correctly? Will we try to troubleshoot problems before calling the vendor's repair service?

So, even when you need to make a capital decision, remember that capital is not the key. People are!

Dear Boss:

Re: Hypocrisy

We understand that rank has its privileges. We expect our bosses to have nicer offices and other perks. And, frankly, we *want* you to have those extras because they are something we'll strive to get—like the proverbial carrot on the end of the stick that keeps us moving forward. So don't get caught up in some egalitarian movement that prescribes that everyone be treated exactly equal. No society, no organization, has ever achieved a true egalitarian setup. Status hierarchies are normal, even necessary.

What bothers us is the hypocrisy that sometimes surrounds these privileges. Our favorite example comes from the last recession. Sales, revenues, and profits all fell. People were actually laid off. You were on a prolonged we-must-cut-costs campaign. Smack in the middle of this crisis, you got your office completely redone—new carpet, curtains, chair, and desk. We're not stupid; we know that redoing an office is a relatively minor expense planned well in advance. The budget cycle probably scheduled the remodeling even before the recession took hold. (Of course, a lot of our laid-off workers also had planned to feed their families and make their house payments before the recession hit!)

The Roman emperor, Marcus Aurelius, saw this issue clearly when he wrote in his *Meditations*: "Never value anything as profitable to thyself which shall compel thee to break thy promise, to lose thy self-respect, to hate any man, to suspect, to curse, to act the hypocrite; to desire anything which needs walls and curtains."

Actions do speak louder than words. Don't tell us one thing (cut costs) and then do another (convert your office into an oasis within a desert of hypocrisy).

The simple question to ask when you are about to benefit, directly or indirectly, is, "How will my employees view this change?"

Dear Boss:

Re: The Great Cash Room

This organization is wealthy and we can prove it. Look around. What do you see? A building, offices, office equipment, computers, company cars, and supplies. This place is a lot bigger and a lot nicer than where we live. Don't tell us about return on investment, profit margins, and cash flow. We know that those buzzwords are merely a smokescreen behind which you plead poverty and avoid giving us more money.

Somewhere, probably connected to the Treasurer's office, we know there's a Great Cash Room. You know, that room that's full of the cash used to finance this place. Obviously, there *must* be a grand stash of cash hidden around here. How else could all these expenses be paid?

We figure that if this organization weren't well-off financially, you would have told us what's going on. You would have brought us into your confidence to win our support. You would have informed us about the organization's performance. Since that hasn't happened, our logical conclusion is that this operation is loaded with money.

Most of us assume that the company earns a margin of 30 or 40 percent. If that sounds high (or low), it is only a guess. To correct our poor guesses and overcome the Great Cash Room Myth, keep us informed about the economic health of the organization. Periodic financial and business briefings would help.

CHAPTER 11
RUNNING OUR DEPARTMENT EFFECTIVELY

Dear Boss:

Re: **Bosses, Managers, and Leaders**

Although we often use the terms *boss, manager,* and *leader* interchangeably, they're really very different. Leaders create a vision around which people rally; managers marshall the resources to achieve this vision. Both are worthy and much-needed roles. And at times managers need to be leaders and vice versa. But bosses are people who lack vision and give orders to cover up their limitations.

When a leader has a vision and shares it, the vision draws enthusiastic commitment out of people like loose metal fillings pulled toward a powerful magnet. People don't need to be motivated because they're pulled toward the vision. The vision motivates them. So leaders rely on the excitement of their visions, managers rely on motivation, and bosses rely on autocratic orders.

What is the vision you hold for us? Around what flagpole do we rally? What does that vision mean to us individually? If the vision isn't translated into a sense of benefit for us—whether it's an appeal to our pride, recognition, or other need—our attraction to it will fade.

As even the Bible (Proverbs 29:18) asserts, "Where there is no vision, the people perish." Without the vision of true leadership, those you lead will vanish; they might stay on the job physically, but their commitment will disappear.

Bosses rely solely on orders, prodding us through directives. So they're neither managers (motivators) nor leaders (visionaries).

Which are you? More important, which do you want to be? Great vision might not spring readily from any of us, but you can emulate great leaders by at least sharing your views on our efforts. They might not form an inspiring vision; nevertheless, sharing whatever views you hold at least lets us believe you're willing to be open with us. And if you're receptive to us, we might be able to help you mold your views into an inspiring vision of what we can become. You can choose to be a boss or a manager or a leader. Which role would you prefer?

Dear Boss:

Re: Problems

Problems are the cutting edge that distinguish between success and failure. Problems call forth our courage and our wisdom; indeed, they create our courage and our wisdom. It is only because of problems that we grow.[9]

The problems we bring you are actually gifts. They offer you the chance to show off your leadership skills and to grow. The mundane, business-as-usual routine might be convenient and even efficient, but it causes little growth. Problems cause discomfort, discomfort causes action, and action to avoid discomfort causes growth.

To say that the problems we bring you are actually gifts does strain credibility in some cases. If we repeatedly create the same problems for you, they're anything but gifts. They benefit neither you nor us.

But excluding repetitive problems, the major leadership glitch that we see is your attitude toward problems. If you could perceive the problems we bring you as opportunities for us to develop, we'd all grow. And after we solve each problem, don't keep bringing it up to remind us of our error. Not only does such moaning pull down our morale, it also reminds us of our shortcomings but does little to build our self-image.

Let's view problems as training opportunities that build morale and challenge our creativity. Use problems as mini-cases and coach us through them to the right answer. We'll learn, grow, and be appreciative.

Dear Boss:

Re: **Delegating vs. Dumping**

When you delegate a responsibility to us, we develop. So keep delegating! Usually you do a good job of assigning duties, granting us authority, and creating in us a sense of responsibility (although your delegation would be even more effective if you checked our comprehension by asking us to explain the task back to you). Nevertheless, you generally recognize that delegated tasks mean more work for us and you acknowledge that feeling, especially when we feel we're being asked to do more than our share. Looking past our whining, you know that when we face a new growth experience, we may hesitate at first, but we feel like better people after we've mastered it.

The real problem arises when you dump work on us because you simply don't want to do it. There's a difference between delegating and dumping! Dumping is when you shovel onto us repetitive, mundane work of little value to either the organization or our growth. Admittedly, grunt work needs to be done. And it makes sense that, as subordinates, we should do it rather than you. But when you hand us the same old stuff over and over, we don't grow—we just get dumped on.

Give us a variety of assignments. If you give us something new, something that stretches us, we'll grow. Don't save all the challenging assignments for yourself. Share them. If you do, we won't mind the grunt work so much. We'll grow, and we'll become more effective. As we become more effective, so will you.

Dear Boss:

Re: Rules and Policies

The fewer rules we have to live with, the easier life is apt to be. The old K.I.S.S. principle—Keep It Simple, Stupid—might be just a cute oversimplification. But we don't need a new rule or policy every time you make a decision. Obviously, when a situation occurs several times, a rule of thumb or even a policy can provide a welcome blueprint. Also, we don't need new rules and policies for the unusual as well as the mundane. In fact the bureaucratic stack of rules and policies we have around here just turns our managers into librarians. Instead of using and developing their judgment, many managers simply look up the answers in policy manuals.

We like the management philosophy of Michael D. Dingman, the creator of Wheelabrator-Frye, Inc., and long-time president of Signal Oil. Here are his management rules: "Keep things simple. Talk straight. Don't hesitate. Ask people what they think. Give people a chance to succeed by themselves."[10] When you layer rule upon rule, policy upon policy, you don't allow us to think. You don't allow us to develop, or to succeed—or fail—by ourselves. Soon we realize that initiative and creativity are less important than compliance with rules and policies. Shortly after that we discover how to manipulate rules and policies to protect us from criticism. Doing the job right becomes less important than following the rules.

Right now you manage and we live in a bureaucracy no one intended to create. If competitors discover how inflexible we are, our next rules and policies might come from a court-appointed administrator.

If we need a new rule or policy, ask us for ideas. We understand the issues, and our input will probably reduce the need for more rules and policies.

Dear Boss:

Re: If It Ain't Broke...

Consider one of the classic business axioms: "If it ain't broke, don't fix it." That sounds reasonable, doesn't it? However, you'll find that axiom at the root of many business problems, even business failures. Why? Because people often turn it into, "If it's working OK, don't improve it. Instead, wait for a competitor to figure out a better way. Then play catch-up at great expense."

The history of General Motors offers a good example. The company's strategy was elegant in its simplicity. Since the end of World War II, GM's highly successful strategy was to sell Chevrolets to the broadest possible cross section of new-car buyers. As these buyers matured and prospered, their goal became to move up to Pontiacs, Buicks, and Oldsmobiles. ("Wouldn't you really rather have a Buick?" And, when they finally arrived, "Isn't it time you had a Cadillac?") What made this strategy so successful for GM was that all five car lines were virtually identical—nicer seats, different sheet metal, and much higher price tags notwithstanding. By using cosmetics and advertising to differentiate their products, GM managed to charge about twice as much for a Cadillac as for a Chevy. The cars were so similar that the courts even made GM announce that we were no longer getting an Olds Rocket 88 engine, but simply one made at a GM plant. So their strategy was really to encourage us to trade up to different sheet metal (although it might cost us twice as much). Besides creation of a profit machine, the result has been more difference between a Chevy Cavalier and a Chevy

Caprice than between the Caprice and a Cadillac Sedan DeVille.

For most of the post-World War II period, the "If it ain't broke, don't fix it" idea was imbedded in GM's strategy. Ford and Chrysler's "me, too" strategy throughout most of the same period allowed them to survive, too. But today, one of every four cars is an import.

Rather than innovating and improving on what they had, Detroit manufacturers decided not to fix what wasn't broken. So one of North America's great industries just wore out. Chrysler, for years the weak sister, even went broke and had to get a bailout from the federal government.

Once they recognized that the manufacturing part of their strategy was, in fact, "broke" the big three began rushing into automation and people programs (while still giving us the same cars at different prices). Since we consumers found out that the companies produced junky cars, they're trying to fix the quality problem. But they still don't see the profitability of their trade-up strategy as broke, so they won't fix it until enough foreign competitors offer a real choice and the automobile executives see their strategy of putting five labels on the same car as broke, too.

If it ain't broke, don't fix it. Wait for a competitor to do it better. Detroit did.

Dear Boss:

Re: **Looking Out vs. Looking In**

A crucial issue any company or department must face is its focus. Do the people focus their attention outward on the contribution they make to others or inward on the internal issues?

When organizational politics and other internal issues become the primary concerns, we often lose sight of our customers, whether the customer is another department or a consumer in the marketplace. This internal focus is heightened by our insecurities. Rampant organizational politics, layoffs, mergers, or other major changes will set the grapevine humming. Receiving and spreading unofficial information becomes a goal in itself. Rumors and personal issues take priority over taking care of our customers. And, of course, the more attention we pay to internal issues the more important these issues seem, demanding an increasing amount of our time and energy.

You can shift the focus back to outside issues by talking about the needs of our customers. Bring us information about their demands; tell us how our actions impact those that use our products or services. No, we won't stop talking about the internal issues, but we'll be able to maintain some perspective. Besides, if someone really needs our contribution, we are likely to feel more confident.

Of course you need to keep us informed about major internal developments, too. If you try to shield us from the facts, we will search them out elsewhere, but if you candidly share your knowledge (not rumors and gossip), you will become our major source of reliable information and our confidence and trust in you will remain. Most important, keep us focused on the outward contribution we are supposed to make. That contribution may be our only anchor during turbulent times.

Dear Boss:

Re: **Guarding Your Turf**

You want us to do the best job we can when it furthers our department's goals. But when we help other parts of the organization, your disdain suggests we're wasting our time. We understand that our department's success is important to you because *your* success rides on it. But why not help out other departments, too?

Sure, the time we devote to helping them might detract from our time for doing our job. We understand that. But your reaction goes much deeper than that. Perhaps you fear the other department will look good, even better than ours. Maybe you're concerned higher-ups will think we're overstaffed if we have time to help others (and perhaps we are!). But if you discourage us from helping others—even through your obvious lack of encouragement—we'll withdraw our assistance. And then, when we need them to pitch in, they won't. Then *we'll* look bad. Worse still, if every department takes the attitude that it's too busy or too understaffed to help the others, that kind of "territoriality" will erect rigid barriers to cooperation. And you know as well as we do that even though the organization chart shows we report *up*, the real work gets done by information flowing *across* the hierarchy. If we erect barriers through a lack of cooperation, the entire organization—including our department—will suffer.

Besides, wouldn't your reputation (and promotability) be enhanced if you were known as someone who looks out for the organization's best interests, always ready to pitch in and help other departments?

Dear Boss:

Re: Power Plays

We want you to know we're aware of the major power tactics people use around this organization. Sometimes we think you're aware of them, too, although you act naive. At other times we fear you *are* naive. For simplicity, we'll call these tactics *emotional, logical,* and *autocratic.*

People who use *emotional* power tactics rely on your wish to be liked. Manners and flattery go a long way here, particularly when people want something from you but have far less power. They know they can't decide the issue. They might even feel unable to influence your decision, so they rely instead on emotional appeals. Usually they begin with flattery and, if that doesn't work, move on to pleading. Emotional power tactics often come from such a low power base that they don't even seem like power tactics, but they are. The power they use comes from artfully playing on your need to be liked.

Logical power plays are just that: they use discussion, rational arguments, explanations (often endless ones), and finally compromises. People who use these tactics can usually talk you to death. They begin with the assumption that we must all be logical and then arrange their words (spoken or written) and symbols (folders, displays, and body language) to leave you two choices—their logical one or some foolish, irrational one. Unlike emotional power tactics, which leave the decision to you, logical tactics let you feel that you're in control even though you're sharing the decision making. And the feeling of shared decision making reassures you that other rational people will also believe your decision is the right one. Of course, should your decision prove to be wrong, you'll notice there's no paper trail that ties the now-illogical decision to the person who persuaded you.

Autocratic power tactics are the *fatal* ones—the ones that don't work. They include giving direct orders, usually with an implied threat to your status, if not your career. These tacticians pride themselves on playing hardball. (By the way, the best way to deal with this approach is to do *exactly* what they order. If you suspend your common sense and do precisely what they tell you, a major mistake will inevitably occur and cause the hardball player to strike out.)

We write you about these power tactics so you'll know that we're aware of the ones you use. We're not asking you to stop using your power. That would be foolish, since all organizations are based on power relationships. But you'll find that most of the time we'll mirror whatever tactics you use: emotional, logical, or autocratic. And, although most of us have heard Lord Acton's observation that "Power tends to corrupt and absolute power corrupts absolutely," we think George Bernard Shaw was more perceptive when he observed, "Power does not corrupt men; fools, however, if they get into a position of power, corrupt power."

CHAPTER 12
HELPING US DO OUR BEST

Dear Boss:

Re: **Perspective**

We want to believe that you care about us, but from our perspective, there is overwhelming evidence that you don't. Never mind whether you really care or not; what matters is how you look from our perspective. Selfish? Self-centered? You bet. But as our boss, you're supposed to consider more than just your own perspective.

We come to doubt that you care primarily because of the way you treat us, especially on issues of trust and communications. We know controls are necessary in any job. After all, you need some way to understand and check on what we're doing, and you need to know whether we're making progress toward our goals. And yet when you impose another control on us without seeking our suggestions or even explaining why we need it, we feel as though you don't trust us.

Communications with you reveal even more about how we're treated. From our perspective, when we tell you about a problem and then nothing happens, you might as well just tell us we don't count. We feel unimportant because, from our perspective, you treated our problems as trivial. Maybe they are. But if you want our dedication, loyalty, and motivation, you must consider how things look from our perspective.

The best way to consider our feelings is to remember that our communications have two sides: the content of what we say and how we feel about it. Our content may be wrong, but we have feelings. Try to validate our feelings even if you must reject our ideas.

Dear Boss:

Re: **The Scrooge Syndrome**

When the name "Scrooge" comes up, we all immediately associate it with someone tightfisted or cheap. But
the story of Scrooge goes much deeper. Sure, Scrooge was
tight, lacking generosity of spirit. However, Charles
Dickens' *A Christmas Carol* also shows how a selfish perspective can be as damaging as financial greed.

Scrooge's tightfistedness seemed appropriate. He
was a businessman and all business people know it's
important to minimize costs; otherwise, profits shrink or
disappear. So on one level his stinginess made sense. But
what Scrooge had failed to do—and what the spirits of
Christmas Past, Present, and Future finally forced him to
do—was look at the implications of his behavior. Sure,
Scrooge was right to reduce costs. His reasons were beyond challenge. However, he failed to see how his behavior affected others. When the spririts pointed out the error
of his ways, he became defensive. He clung to his reasons
and, since his reasons were solid, he used them to justify
his actions.

Similarly, whenever you challenge one of our
cherished ideas, we cling desperately to our reasons and
justifications to defend our egos. Somehow we believe we
can hide behind our reasons—which you often correctly
identify as mere excuses. And sometimes when you hide
behind your logic or reasons, you also fail to consider the
consequences of your actions. Often you have sound reasons for your actions but don't consider the consequences
for us. If you want a loyal, committed, and motivated work

force, show us your empathy by looking at both the reasons for *and* the impacts of your behavior. Consider not just your logic, but also its consequences for us.

Perhaps George Bernard Shaw said it best: "The man who listens to Reason is lost: Reason enslaves all whose minds are not strong enough to master her."

Sure, Scrooge was right in trying to save money. He simply forgot that feelings are often more important than reasons. It's unlikely that some spirit is going to show you the consequences of your behavior, so you'll need to become more aware on your own.

Dear Boss:

Re: **Assumptions**

We all simplify the world by making assumptions. On these assumptions we build our beliefs about the people around us. So when our assumptions are wrong, our beliefs are wrong, too. And our assumptions shape how we treat people.

What do you actually assume about each of us? Think about it. Your assumptions determine how you deal with us.

When you give orders, your behavior suggests we can't think for ourselves. (Sometimes we stop thinking for ourselves intentionally and follow your orders *exactly*, just for the amusement we get when things go wrong. So you see, we *can* think!) If you want our cooperation, assume that we have something to contribute, even if it's only our enthusiasm. Tell us the objective, if we don't already know it, and then assume we're bright enough to figure out how to achieve it. And assume we're bright enough to ask for help if we need it.

Ask us what we think; don't assume we're dummies. We're not perfect, but we usually know how to get the job done. If you have any doubts, ask us how we'll go about it. When we follow *your* orders, we're denied feelings of accomplishment. You achieve; we work. Let us achieve, too, by assuming we have something to contribute. If you do, we'll be more motivated. If you assume we can't handle more responsibility, you give us little opportunity to develop.

You see, your assumptions are self-fulfilling because you base your actions on them. For example, the cycle of low motivation begins with your assumptions about our motivation. Want proof? Think back about how enthusiastic each of us was when first hired. What happened to that enthusiasm? Where did it go? It was buried under the assumptions you made about us. We lived up to—or, more correctly, down to—your assumptions.

Your assumptions affect a lot more than just our motivation, too. You control the valve through which we receive information. The size of the opening is determined by your assumptions about us, by how much you trust us. Your self-fulfilling assumptions about our low worth close the valve, and you share little information with us. Since we get little information, we assume you don't care, so we respond in kind. And then we notice how the control systems and security measures around here are also filled with the assumptions you and others hold about us.

Plato said that people are beings in search of meaning. When you base your behavior on assumptions that we're lazy or dumb, you deny us the chance to make a meaningful contribution. We're all reasonable people. We might not have as much experience or education as you do, but that doesn't mean we're stupid. Figure out how you want us to perform; then adjust your assumptions to match. If you do that, *your* behavior will begin a self-fulfilling prophecy: you'll create a highly dedicated, loyal, and motivated work force.

Dear Boss:

Re: **The Machiavellian Trap**

Fearing that other people are better can lead into two traps. The first is to surround yourself with people whom you don't see as threats. One boss we had, for example, hired people without college degrees; figuring none of them would be promoted, he felt safe. Of course, when a couple of us went to night school, he tried to remove the threat by transferring us to other departments. And after that he tried to hire only young, single, or recently married women, apparently hoping they would leave their jobs for marriage or family.

The second trap is the divide-and-conquer strategy. Another boss we had divided up work among us in such a way that none of us knew the entire department's role— so, presumably, none of us would be capable of replacing him.

Both these ex-bosses feared losing their jobs. Intentionally or not, their own superiors must have followed the dictums of Niccolò Machiavelli, who wrote more than 400 years ago in *The Prince* that "since love and fear can hardly exist together, if we must choose between them, it is far safer to be feared than loved."

The trap our previous bosses fell into was to apply the same logic to us that their own bosses were applying to them. They tried to motivate us with fear. Initially our performance probably improved, reinforcing their misconception that fear was an effective tool. As they applied more pressure, however, many people quit. The rest of us took refuge in our narrowly defined jobs, doing *exactly* as we were told. Productivity dropped, and we finally got a new, less paranoid boss.

The irony of the Machiavellian approach is that it creates the situation every boss fears: poor performance. Bosses become trapped by their own efforts because Machiavellian approaches do ultimately lead to poor performance. Then, by the time the department's performance becomes unacceptably poor, we workers are too drained to rally around and save our boss with extra effort. Besides, even if we wanted to pitch in, the divide-and-conquer approach has kept us too ignorant to help.

Treat us like allies and you can easily avoid this trap. Your efforts to develop us, train us, and make us even better than you will energize us with enthusiasm and loyalty.

Dear Boss:

Re: Fostering Creativity

Some of our competitors have lower costs, new equipment, or other advantages. So how are we going to compete with them?

A common first reaction is to say, "Work harder!" If we did, we'd get more done at a lower cost. But if we work harder today, what do we do to improve performance tomorrow? Work still harder? Obviously, we have limits to how hard we can work. But there are no limits on *creativity*. If we're more creative than our competitors, we gain an advantage over them. Even if they copy us, we can find another creative solution the next day. We can simply be more and more creative. If, on the other hand, our competitors become more creative, they'll overtake us regardless of who has lower costs or newer equipment.

Everyone can be creative. Sure, some of us are more creative than others. But every person has some degree of creativity. Want proof? Imagine if you told us that every employee must come up with a creative idea next week—and would get $100,000 for it—or would be fired. What do you think would happen? We bet you'd be buried under ideas! But if so many creative ideas exist, why don't you hear about them now? Because you don't have $100,000 bonuses to give away? Maybe, but we think you can get our ideas without buying them.

To be creative we need to combine existing resources in new ways to solve problems. But to solve problems, we need to believe we have the authority to solve them and that you appreciate our efforts.

We know that every idea we come up with isn't a winner. In fact some are downright impractical, even dumb. But when you criticize our ideas you sometimes kill our creativity as surely as though you had shot it. The most common creativity killers around here are these:

Penalize us for taking a risk. Sure, if we take a risk and fail, you can't just brush it aside. You might even need to take corrective action to make sure we don't take the same risk again. But when you do, be sure you also let us know you do want us to continue taking risks. Punish our mistakes, but don't punish us for taking risks. Otherwise we'll stop trying, and progress in our area will stop, too.

Cover yourself above all else. When we see you covering yourself by writing memos to the file or transcribing phone conversations, you send us a message of paranoia. Not only do we worry about your fears, we also see this place as more fearful than it needs to be. Fear doesn't stimulate us toward creativity—except in covering our trail.

Don't encourage our ideas. Most good ideas come from rough ones being transformed by the enthusiastic interest of others. If we bring up an idea and you act indifferent, our creative juices freeze. We need your enthusiasm, perhaps even bordering on the effusive, as the antifreeze to keep our creative ideas flowing.

Do you really want our creativity? If so, challenge us! *Ask* for our suggestions. Ask for them again and again until we come up with usable ideas. After you ask, *listen;* listen carefully to our thoughts. As you listen, realize that our suggestions aren't perfectly thought out yet. So, instead of trying to shoot holes in our ideas, help us refine them into a creative solution. If the ideas are no good, that will become obvious as you coach us. But once you get practical solutions, *use* them. Using our ideas is the best reinforcement you can provide (although do feel free to add some praise, too).

Dear Boss:

Re: Initiative

Some bosses fail to realize that our initiative and results from our initiative are two separate matters. What happens when we show initiative around here? When we do and we make a mistake, you criticize, which discourages *both* our effort and our initiative. Show us that you appreciate our initiative, especially when our efforts go wrong. Otherwise, we learn quickly that initiative and punishment go hand in hand. As a result, our initiative declines.

Too often our initiative meets with criticism even when ninety-nine percent of what we did was right; the one percent is nitpicked, second-guessed, or simply criticized. The result? An *inevitable* lack of initiative. Finally, don't use yourself as an example by saying that you yourself respond to criticism by working harder. Maybe you do. But we tend to withdraw from actions that are likely to draw criticism. And criticism sticks to initiative around here like white on rice.

Do you want to foster initiative? If so, please remember to split our initiatives into two parts: the initiative and the results. Don't forget to praise us for taking initiative, even if the results are wrong. Otherwise, in our minds we'll lump both parts together, and we'll stop initiating. When you recognize our efforts, regardless of the results, we'll be more likely to come back with new ideas.

Dear Boss:

Re: **Uncorking Our Talent**

John Huston, the Academy Award–winning director and actor, once commented on working with actors. He often told such actors as Albert Finney, "'Work something out; I'll leave you alone.' I'd leave them for an hour or two and they'd come up with something."[11] Consider also the view of the long-time Chairman of the Board at General Motors, Roger B. Smith: "We've got to cut out bureaucracy, eliminate redundancy, and make more efficient use of our people. And probably most important of all, *we've got to uncork individual talent*...by giving our people the opportunity to take risks, assume responsibility...and earn rewards."[12]

We could add a hundred more such quotes. The point, however, is simple and straightforward: no matter whether you're dealing with actors, automobile workers, or office workers, we all have talents and skills. Let us use them! Challenge us for our ideas and then use them. Sure, errors will result. But we don't exist to avoid errors, we exist to accomplish something.

As John Akers observed after becoming president and CEO of IBM Corporation: "If you want people to step forward and lead the parade—especially a parade into new and unchartered territory—then you can't fire everyone who leads it slightly off course. You have to believe in people, and you have to give them more than one chance."[13]

If we're not making *enough* errors, that means we're not stretching far enough.

CHAPTER 13
TRAINING AND CAREER DEVELOPMENT

Dear Boss:

Re: Orientation

The orientation of a new employee takes time—yours and ours. It also seems as though we are always very busy when a new employee arrives to begin work. (In fact, we are usually busy because we are shorthanded, which is why we hired the new person in the first place.) As a result, orientation—at least at the department level—is, at best, a hit-or-miss arrangement when it should be a rare opportunity for you and us.

At no other time will you have a better opportunity to open lines of communication with new employees. The new recruits are free from the distortions of the peer group; they haven't formed many opinions about the job, company, or boss; and they're especially eager to please their boss (a feeling quickly quashed by many peer groups). Never will the opportunity for open, two-way communications be better.

What an effective orientation can do is win over new employees to the boss's view of the job and the company. The boss can explain the rationale for job layout and design. And the boss can stress the importance of efficiency, quality, and safety without making the employees feel defensive.

For the new employees, orientation can help reduce their initial anxieties about the job and the social setting. If they're less anxious about whether they will fit in, they're better able to focus on learning their job. Less anxiety also means fewer of the newcomers are likely to quit.

At Texas Instruments, managers found that an effective orientation for newly hired production workers resulted in not only lower turnover, but also faster learning times. The orientation paid off twice.

Right now the sink-or-swim mentality dominates this organization. We believe everyone would benefit from a more effective orientation program—a program that acquaints all newcomers with our people, place, policies, and procedures in addition to the traditionally discussed fringe benefits.

If you supplemented the orientation with a buddy system, integrating new employees would be smoother and less costly—both emotionally and financially. To add a buddy system to our orientation efforts, all you'd need to do is ask one of us to help orient each newcomer. Ask us to take the new person under our wing. We'd be flattered you asked and it would give the newcomer a psychological home base.

Dear Boss:

Re: The Sink-or-Swim Mentality

This company has a real macho mind-set. People are put into strange situations and basically told to sink or swim. And a lot of people around here approve of that philosophy. The so-called logic is this: "The sink-or-swim philosophy is the fastest way to see if a person can make it around here. Besides, that's how I learned the ropes."

Certainly the sink-or-swim approach is a fast way to evaluate whether someone can make it. But is our goal to see how fast we can evaluate someone's potential? Or is it to *benefit* from their potential? If our goal is only to evaluate quickly, even at the expense of overlooking their long-term potential, then the sink-or-swim method is probably best. However, if we want to get their maximum potential contribution, we need to change our approach.

Consider what happens to transfers moved under the sink-or-swim approach. After—at best—very little orientation and training, they're expected to perform. Asking co-workers is their only real way to learn the ropes because asking you, the boss, might make them look incapable. So our own productivity is interrupted as we try to explain our procedures in a haphazard, even random, way. Maybe transfers and new-hires learn the jobs and maybe they don't. But regardless of the outcome, can you really defend this approach on the grounds of efficiency?

But if this sink-or-swim approach is really such a poor way of finding out what a person has to give, why does it persist? On one level it does seem to be a definitive test, each newcomer does either sink or swim. Proof of success or failure is clear and needs no interpretation. And for those who swim, they know they did it on their own.

But we suspect there's a more fundamental reason why this approach persists. We think the sink-or-swim mentality is really a way for bosses to abdicate responsibility for new employees or employees in new roles. It means that you can wash your hands of any responsibility for the outcome. If a person fails—as many do—you can always say, "It's good we found that out so quickly," or else blame "those people in personnel who can't hire good people." Either way you're absolved of responsibility. Of course, transferred employees' and newcomers' chances for success would be higher if you became involved. But that would mean not only a demand on your time, but also personal involvement. You'd be at least partially responsible for the outcome.

We can make life easier for transfers and new hires by giving them a solid orientation and a buddy, as described in the previous memo. Then we could add some training. Orientation and training combined with our special efforts to learn of their problems would increase their chances for a smooth transition.

Dear Boss:

Re: **59-Second Supervisors**

    You say it so quickly as you walk away: "I'm very glad to inform you of your promotion to supervisor. Let me be the first to congratulate you and shake your hand. We're sure you'll be a great supervisor and do a good job. Your long years of service, your knowledge of our operations, and your dedication mean you can't miss in this new job. If you ever have any questions, come see me. My door is always open. But I'm sure you won't have any problems. Once again, congratulations and good luck!"

    One moment one of us is just another worker, and 59 seconds later that person is a supervisor. We all know the differences between being a good worker and being a good supervisor. But *becoming* a good supervisor takes more than a handshake, a pat on the back, and a few reassuring words. From time to time we're going to need to promote people to supervisory positions. And those supervisors are going to be responsible for tens of thousands of dollars in salaries, materials, and, ultimately, customer goodwill. So why is their entire training program limited to the 59-second ritual depicted in the first paragraph?

    You can begin to prepare us to be supervisors before you promote us. Supervisory training sessions, job rotations, delegations, special projects, and some coaching *before* promoting us could make the process much more effective.

Dear Boss:

Re: Maintaining People vs. Machines

We're amused by the difference between the way people and machines are treated. Take, for example, a $100,000 piece of equipment. Before we buy it, we need a capital budget approval. Then we contact multiple vendors and carefully review their machines. We discuss financing and finally make the decision. Then we follow our purchase decision with a detailed maintenance schedule to which we adhere rigidly. (We can just hear you saying, "It had *better* be well maintained. After all, it cost $100,000!")

But consider what happens when we hire new employees. Often the people we hire are the first ones we interview. They get no orientation, little training, and are left to sink or swim. If the new-hire makes it or fails, so be it. No one puts together a maintenance schedule for further training, follow-up orientations, planned counseling sessions, or systematic feedback (unless the employee is doing poorly, of course).

The irony is that a $15,000 car or a $100,000 machine is cheap compared to a new employee! Even a minimum-wage employee costs around $10,000 a year if you include benefits. More skilled employees cost several times that much. If you consider that an employee might work here for twenty years, that $10,000 figure quickly balloons to $200,000. If you go one step further and consider the value of equipment and materials that one employee can impact during a career, you need to add many more hundreds of thousands to the real cost.

So where is the maintenance schedule for this valuable human resource? People are valuable assets—often worth hundreds of thousands of dollars—so we'd like to propose that you set up a maintenance schedule. It should have several parts, including regularly scheduled performance reviews. For new employees, those reviews should be positive and informal, occurring several times during the first month. Then monthly reviews would be useful for at least the first six months. After this break-in period, we recommend standard performance evaluations every six months.

Positive reinforcement for nearly everything the newcomer does right must be a high priority. Random compliments (recognition for good work) should be most frequent during the first few months, and continue periodically thereafter.

Of course we must take corrective action whenever needed. But, most important, we should build the employees' confidence with positive feedback through regularly scheduled maintenance and periodic compliments.

Dear Boss:

Re: Training Programs

Training programs can be either the best or the worst use of our time. Whether a program ends up being a boon or a boondoggle depends on how much of the training gets *applied*. If we come back with new ideas and you condemn them as "not the way we do things around here," our time and the organization's money have been wasted. The information remains trapped in the classroom, not transferred to the job. That kind of training squanders resources.

On the other hand, you can make training cost effective. First, ask us what we learned. That action alone will force us to pay more attention in future classes because we know you'll ask. We've even seen managers who ask for a one-page summary and evaluation of the session.

Next, be open to the ideas we pick up. Perhaps they're not always appropriate, but encourage us to use what we can. If the material isn't useful, we'll know. And if we find useful applications, they'll reinforce our learning and help us transfer the knowledge from the classroom to the job.

Finally, follow up to see how the new knowledge affects our abilities, skills, or attitudes. If the results are positive, encourage us to use the new-found ideas. Both you and the organization will get a lot more out of our training budget!

Dear Boss:

Re: Helping Us Develop

We've tried to avoid comparing you directly with previous bosses because we don't like people comparing us. Nevertheless, we want to tell you the story of a boss we'll call "Roger."

Roger held a job very similar to yours, and he had both good and bad points as a boss. One of his exceptional characteristics was his view of developing his subordinates. He felt that developing his people was second only to doing his job. As he often said, "If I develop my people, they'll do my job; they'll assure my success." He was right!

Roger's unswerving dedication to our development began with his critical examination of our performance. When we left performance review sessions with him, we felt like we'd been under a high-powered microscope. Sometimes he knew more about our performance than we did. He could recite, in considerable detail, examples of *both* good and poor performance since our last review. And when we left, regardless of whether our performance had been great or poor, we felt all revved up. His review sessions were not witch hunts. But Roger really knew our strengths and our weaknesses.

Part of the reason why we felt so fired up was that he would end each session by discussing our career plans and offering constructive help. Often, if we were doing our jobs acceptably, he would suggest some developmental idea. Sometimes he'd suggest formal education, such as another degree or a certification course. At other times he'd propose a specific training session or a task force assignment. His favorite developmental tool, however, was old-fashioned job rotation.

Once people in Roger's department had pretty much mastered their jobs, he saw no reason for them to keep doing the same thing. Many times he'd say, "Redoing a job you've learned doesn't further your career." For some people who were going to night school or had family concerns, a stable, already-mastered job was ideal. Roger would honor their requests to stay in the jobs they'd mastered, if they had good reasons. But in general, once people had mastered their jobs, Roger was ready to move them on, usually laterally. But his movements were not just for movement's sake. He often explained why a move was needed to balance out a person's experience: "This move will make you a more attractive candidate for promotions here or back to the home office." And so, with our consent he'd move us until we mastered the next job. We never had time to go stale. We were always challenged. He'd even rotate secretaries with production workers so each saw what the other did.

The odd thing about Roger's dedication was it meant a heavy administrative burden for him. Since so many people were new at their jobs, he often needed to help them come up to speed. In short, his concern for our careers created additional work for him. And yet he continued to push for our development.

One real benefit of Roger's dedication was hope. Each of us was always growing, and we knew that our growth would be rewarded by still more new assignments. We all had hope for a better future. Sure, sometimes over lunch we'd yearn for a nice, routine, mundane, well-mastered job. But none of us really wanted such a stagnant existence. Besides, if one of us ever felt overtaxed, Roger would be there pitching in or insisting we take a long vacation while he filled in.

His single-minded dedication to our growth held another mixed blessing for Roger. The bad news (for him, not us) was that a high proportion of his people were promoted, either within our operation or back to the home office. That meant temporary staff shortages. It also meant Roger had to train new people, since he tried to avoid rotating us back into jobs we'd held previously.

The good news was two-fold. First, imagine our dedication to Roger! We felt motivated to get the job done right the first time in order to make him look good. We *owed* him. Sure, we knew he'd eventually get promoted and we'd lose him. But we figured he'd simply be in a higher-level position and would still look out for our careers. People performed for Roger. And if some people did drag their feet, the peer pressure was subtle at first but eventually became merciless (which explains why really poor performers tended to improve quickly or resign).

The other good news for Roger was the network he created throughout the company. Because so many of his people were promoted to higher positions, either here or back at headquarters, he has an international grapevine of well-informed people—people who owe him a favor. Rumor has it that home-office executives call Roger to learn the latest news about the company. In fact, one old-timer said that Roger could retire and live off the free meals: when he's back at the home office, everybody wants to take him to lunch.

Dedication to subordinates begets dedication back. And along with that dedication comes loyalty and hard work. Not only do employees feel cared for, they also have a reason to care for the boss. We all want to care for our bosses; we just need a reason. Roger, through his never-ending insistence that we grow and develop, showed he cared for us. And his fast rise through the company demonstrates we all cared about him.

Dear Boss:

Re: **Victims**

Victims often contribute to their positions, at least in some measure. Their contribution—whether it's resignation to their situation, lack of preparation, or a simple lack of assertiveness—leads to a common reaction: blame the victim. Any struggle leaves casualties. But for there to be victims, there must also be victimizers. Most unfortunately, the victims usually are those least able to help themselves—people who feel underqualified or stuck in dead-end jobs.

Victims are people who don't know they have choices. They might well have options of which they're unaware. But as long as they perceive that they have few if any options, they remain victims.

As a boss you can help by finding—even creating—options for people who are victims. Identify new career paths, explain new ways they can look at their situations, create growth opportunities for them through training or job rotation, or find new ways for them to contribute. No one is in a better position than you are to create options so that these people can regain a favorable self-image, grow beyond their current limits, and feel good about both themselves and their contributions to our organization.

When you create choices for others, you also create choices for yourself. As the previous memo on "Helping Us Develop" explained more fully, you'll create loyal allies while improving the performance of those around you. Converting victims into allies benefits them, the organization, and you. Besides our competitors, who can lose?

Dear Boss:

Re: Secretaries

Secretaries around here are generally outside the career flow. They get secretarial jobs and that's where their careers end. Period. Oh, they might move up and become executive secretaries if they hitch their careers to the right bosses. Occasionally a secretary might even swing a transfer to elsewhere in the organization. But in general, once they're secretaries, that's where they're stuck. And that's unfortunate for several reasons, some obvious and some not.

First, it's just plain unfair to assign someone to a category and leave them there. Yes, we're aware that some people don't want to leave their secretarial jobs; they enjoy the work and might even have gained considerable power by association. In fact some would even quit if you asked them to do another job. You know as well as we do, however, that some secretaries are as bright—(or even brighter)—than their bosses, but they would never request a job transfer for fear of appearing disloyal. So there they sit. And when the issue of immobile secretaries comes up, many bosses blame them—the victims.

Instead of just letting them sit there, or worse, blaming them for their situation, why not take action? Suggest further training or formal education. Point out, even encourage them to pursue, career opportunities. Guide them. Again, we know the obvious answer: you'd lose a valuable secretary. But would you? Or would you gain a very valuable ally now in a key job? Even if your secretary moved to a totally different department, you'd still have a contact, an ally. If you were even partially responsible for this person's new-found success, you'd always find goodwill upon which to draw.

Our organization would benefit, too. Former secretaries would start with a unique base of contacts and information from the informal organization. And as explained more fully in the memo, "Degrees," they would find themselves at job levels unlikely in other organizations. Low turnover and great loyalty to the organization would result.

Besides, imagine the motivational benefits your efforts would have before the transfer or promotion even took place. Sensing your exceptional concern, your secretary would respond with even better performance. Dedication breeds dedication. And of course your secretary would have lots of positive things to say about you on the secretarial grapevine. Do you think other secretaries would be eager to work with you once yours left? You bet! And in the meantime, you'd be held in higher esteem by other secretaries, those gatekeepers of access to information.

Offer our secretaries *careers*, not just jobs. They'll benefit, the organization will benefit, and so will you.

Dear Boss:

Re: Your Replacement

Years ago there was one of those office jokes that was photocopied and spread around. We don't remember who came up with it and we can't remember the exact phrasing of this little poem. But the gist was to have people who think they're really important to the organization stick their hands in a bucket of water. They can even splash the water and move their hands around. But, if they really want to know how much they would be missed, all they have to do is pull their hands out of the water and watch for a few moments. The size of the hole that remains shows how much they would be missed.

Guess what? This organization would go on without you, too. So since you're replaceable, no matter how much you try to splash around and make yourself seem irreplaceable, why not take advantage of your replaceability?

Imagine what would happen if you worked to groom a replacement. This wouldn't need to be an exercise in playing favorites. You could groom the obvious replacement or, failing that, help groom several of us. Competition among several of us striving to learn your job would be stimulating. We'd all grow. With luck some of us might even get promoted into other departments.

We know what you're thinking: why should I want to make it easier for someone to replace me? Because if you were truly irreplaceable, you wouldn't be promotable! If, on the other hand, you were truly replaceable, you'd also be promotable.

You are probably also thinking, "Why should I groom potential replacements for other departments or divisions?" Putting in all that effort and then losing the person does seem like a waste of time, especially if the person goes to work for a competitor, either within the firm or beyond. True. But just for a moment imagine what would happen to motivation around here if people believed you were committed to furthering their careers. Do you think motivation would improve? What about morale? Would these people produce extra effort? Even if they did leave, so what? All that would mean is that you'd have another ally, one who might be able to help you from time to time while singing your praises in the meantime. What would happen to your career if you became known as a developer of solid talent? Wouldn't junior executives and trainees eagerly seek out your guidance? Wouldn't your influence be enhanced?

Even if your potential replacement quit and went to work for a competitor, you would have a personal link to the "enemy." The insights you gained might make you an even more effective leader. Besides, having allies in the industry would be particularly useful should you ever leave here, voluntarily or involuntarily. Perhaps we're not being very logical to suggest how you might benefit at the company's expense. But we believe (albeit selfishly) that you *and* the company would benefit greatly if you became a mentor to us.

CHAPTER 14
FOSTERING HIGH MORALE

Dear Boss:

Re: **Pride and Performance**

Those of us who have pride in our work, in our boss, and in our organization must perform well. We don't want to fall short because we respect what our organization and our boss stand for. We strive to live up to the proud image we carry around in our heads. We feel reasonably assured that if we perform well, we'll be able to stay with an organization and boss that bring us pride, both directly and vicariously. Perhaps Churchton Collins said it best: "Though pride is not a virtue, it is the parent of many virtues."

When we lack pride in you or our organization, our "Why bother?" attitude usually leads to poor performance. Sure, some of us view ourselves as professionals or have high inner standards, so our performance doesn't slip. But for most of us it's hard to value our contribution highly when we lack pride in you and the organization.

All our concern for pride puts you in an awkward position. If you run down our organization, directly or indirectly, by putting down its policies, procedures, or people, you undermine our pride. Worse yet, we might agree with you and develop a case of selective perception, which would enable us to find our own reasons for losing pride. On the other hand, if you act like a Polyanna, your credibility plummets, which also makes it hard for us to have pride in you.

If you're faced with something clearly negative regarding the organization, you might try acknowledging it and then asking how we can make it better. But however you handle it, don't undermine our pride in this place. If you do, you might undo our team spirit, our sense of unity. As longshoreman-turned-philosopher Eric Hoffer observed, "The greatest endeavor in which the masses most readily unite is basically in the search for pride."

Dear Boss:

Re: The "People Are the Same" Myth

Just because we all hold the same jobs with the same job title, that doesn't mean we're all the same. We each differ in many ways. If you see us as interchangeable, you stop treating us as individuals and start treating us as members of a herd.

Even putting aside our own feelings, we believe this approach has real dangers for you. You see, once you start thinking of us as an undifferentiated herd, it's only a small step to depreciating our individual worth. And once you see our individual worth as unimportant, then your treatment of us becomes unimportant, too. Petty bosses build their own egos by putting their employees down. Deprive us of our dignity and worth, and mistreating us might easily follow.

Why, for example, do you think soldiers develop slang terms—"Rebs," "Krauts," and the like? By denigrating the enemy it becomes easier to kill them. Suddenly you're no longer killing your own kind—other "God-fearing Christians," for example. Instead you're shooting indistinguishable members of a herd you called by whatever derogatory term happens to be in vogue.

We know no one is killing our clerk-typists or production workers. But when you see us workers as part of a group, it becomes easier to be inconsiderate, whether it's in scheduling last-minute overtime or layoffs the week before Christmas.

Sure, many of us do the same job. And maybe the work is so carefully structured it takes little training or intelligence to do. But treating us all the same is starting down a stairway that puts employee relations in the cellar. And once we're down there, the stairway back to good morale and high productivity is steep and not easy to climb.

Dear Boss:

Re: **Are We Having Fun Yet?**

Bertrand Russell once observed, "a sense of duty is useful in work but offensive in personal relations."

When you do something for us—whether it's giving us a raise or taking us out to lunch—don't act like you're *supposed* to do it. Do it as though you're *glad* to do it. Show us you're enjoying the situation, not just going through the motions.

Notice, for example, how most of the executives act at the annual picnic. With only a couple of exceptions, they all arrive late, mingle (briefly and in an obligatory way) with the troops, stand around and talk with each other and their spouses, look at their watches a lot, and leave early. You can almost feel their discomfort. Sure, part of their concern is that they're out of their corporate uniforms and probably feel exposed. And part of it is feeling vulnerable, too, since we're all more willing to open up about our complaints after a few beers. But the overall impression they create is that they're attending only out of a sense of duty. Sometimes we want to walk up to them and ask, "Are we having fun yet?"

Much of your job consists of obligations such as punctuality or attendance at the company picnic. But, if you will set a positive example, show a smile, you will help us all cheer up. We've noticed that a positive attitude, even at the company picnic, makes those obligations more fun than just going through the motions.

Dear Boss:

Re: **Rituals**

We know that you think some of our little rituals are silly, even counterproductive. But no matter whether they're birthday parties, baby showers, or goodbye parties for people who leave, these rituals do serve a purpose. They make our job setting more humane. Work has to be more than just work; it has a social dimension, too. Pulling together socially bonds the group into a more cohesive unit. And cohesion, in turn, reduces turnover, even absenteeism. When each of us feels like a part of the group, we don't want to let the others down by quitting or calling in sick. Besides, we spend nearly a quarter of every week at work, so shouldn't we note personal milestones? Why shouldn't work be as humane as possible?

Our rituals serve as useful symbols, helping us to mark changes in our work environment. We need these rituals as reference points similar to graduation or marriage ceremonies, which signal major changes in our personal lives.

Dear Boss:

Re: **Favoritism**

Favoritism is not a comfortable topic for us to discuss with you, particularly since we're not your favorites. It's probably not an easy issue for you either, unless you've fooled yourself into thinking you don't play favorites. You do. All bosses do, even the very best. What really good bosses do, however, is recognize favoritism and do their very best to minimize it.

We know that personnel policies, past practices, and pressures from other people greatly limit your flexibility. You have less control over raises, for example, than you'd like. So how do you reward people who do a truly superb job? How do you let them know you appreciate their extra efforts or cooperation?

You do it in myriad ways, some obvious and some subtle. If you see several of your favorites standing around telling jokes, you join in. But when some of us who aren't your favorites do that, you glare at us as if to say, "Work!" When we're late, we hear about it; when we call in sick, you treat us suspiciously. You always assign opportunities to fill in for an absent employee and learn a new job (and become more promotable) to your favorites—unless, of course, it's a job no one enjoys. We always get them! And we don't even want to talk about how you handle assignment of overtime, because it, too, is another example of your favoritism.

Still, you face the question, "How can I reward good performers, given the limited discretion I have?" And that question is at the heart of the problem. By showing favoritism to those who work harder, you do encourage their hard work. But at the same time you create resentment among the rest of us who don't receive your little perks. Then we try to see how little work we can do. It might be immature of us to react like spoiled children and cut back on our efforts but, nevertheless, that's what seems to happen. Your favorites, spurred on by your encouragement, work harder, further widening the gap between their performance and ours. More rewards for them are followed by further withdrawal by us. Resentment builds, morale drops.

Sure, you should reward good performers. Give them bigger raises or other forms of recognition. But don't show favoritism by letting them come in late or leave early while rigidly enforcing our working hours. That's favoritism. Either chew all of us out for being late or none of us, but be consistent. Rotate the good *and* the bad jobs. If someone is doing more work—and we know that better than you do—give them a larger merit increase or some other formal award. But, don't show favoritism just because you like them.

You might do well to remember what Niccolò Machiavelli observed: "Friendships that are won by awards, and not by greatness and nobility of soul, although deserved, are not real, and cannot be depended upon in time of adversity." You still can't buy loyalty or friends; you have to earn them through your day-to-day treatment of all of us.

Dear Boss:

Re: **Selective Perception**

Has it ever struck you that when you buy a new car, you start to notice that model a lot more as you drive around? It's almost as if hundreds suddenly appeared overnight. Or try closing your eyes and listening to the various sounds around you right now that you've been filtering out.

The human mind cannot notice everything; the result would be information overload. So we filter out most of what goes on, only noticing either the truly unusual or what we're sensitized to perceive. Buying a new car, for example, sensitizes us to that make and model. Our involvement in choosing and buying the car sensitizes us, so we perceive that model selectively, quite out of proportion to its actual popularity on the roads.

Selective perception also applies to your management style. Let's assume, for example, that you used to show favoritism to one employee in your department. After a while you realized how damaging that was to our group's morale and motivation. So you immediately cut out all the favoritism and began treating that person exactly like you treat all of us. Exactly. Several months pass, and now we're all in a group meeting. Your ex-favorite makes a suggestion, a very good one, and you publicly acknowledge it as a good idea. No favoritism is intended nor does any exist. Yet, because of our selective perception, we're likely to see your acknowledgement as further evidence of your on-going favoritism. Why? Since we had noticed your favoritism earlier, we're extremely sensitive to anything that even appears to be favoritism. Then, when you make a perfectly normal comment—one you might say to any of us—our selective perception leads us to see your comment as further proof of your favoritism. We perceive the situation selectively.

Once we develop a perception on any topic, not just favoritism, it needs to be reinforced only occasionally to keep it alive. The point for you as a boss is an important one: you must consider your actions not just in terms of reality, but in terms of how they get filtered through our selective perceptions. Moreover, when you're dealing with ultra-sensitive issues such as favoritism, you must be particularly aware of our selective perception.

Dear Boss:

Re: Negativism

We all get frustrated from time to time, and we do need to release our frustration. It seems, though, that being negative is rewarded around here. Whenever any of us says something negative about another person or department, they're usually reassured and seldom rebuked. Most of the time just announcing that we have a problem with some other person or department causes our co-workers to agree, often adding their own criticism. Their agreement or, even better, their added anecdotes, reinforce our naysaying. The critic not only has center stage, but also gets validated by the supporting comments. And that process of validation by our peers encourages even more negativism.

That sort of negativism needs to be rebuked by you, our boss. If you serve as a role model by standing up to the negative whining we hear, we'll all start to realize that we don't need to automatically agree with every critic. We think the best way to change the negative attitude around here is simply to ask each critic, "What do you think we should *do* about your criticism?" If you make it clear that you expect criticism to lead to action, people will be more selective about what they criticize. And when they do criticize, everyone will expect them to take action.

Dear Boss:

Re: Positivism

Do you get enough positive feedback from your boss? Well, we feel as if we don't get enough from you. Give us more positive feedback, and we'll give you a more motivated performance.

Can you help us create a more positive atmosphere? Negativity occurs in all organizations; a certain amount is probably normal. What we really need is positive behavior to counterbalance the negative. We all need to search for positive aspects of our jobs, organization, customers, and co-workers. And, when we find positives, we need to share them. As our boss, you can help us by taking the lead in being positive and sharing positive observations.

It's axiomatic that none of us can be expected to have a more positive attitude than you do. You know more than we do about what's going on around here, so if you're negative, we follow. Your attitude, positive or negative, is particularly contagious. As suggested in the book, *The One-Minute Manager*, a boss should try to catch us doing something right.[14] Find reasons to pat us on the back, figuratively speaking. Reward us for our good behavior, even though that's the behavior you expect.

Positivism goes beyond just recognizing us for doing a good job. Your recognition should extend to our ideas. Usually you greet our ideas or suggestions with negative comments: "Have you considered...?" or, "We tried that back when...." Or else you hit us with scores of questions to pick the ideas apart. No, you shouldn't blindly accept our ideas. But what would happen if you asked yourself, "What's good about the idea?"

Sure, you face limitations in using our ideas. And a particular idea might not even be feasible. But does it have the seeds of a good idea? What parts of it *would* work? What changes might make this idea a blockbuster success? If you approached each employee idea positively, seeing limitations only as prods to creativity and imagination, what would happen to morale and motivation? Try adopting Frank Lloyd Wright's viewpoint: "The human race built most nobly when limitations were greatest and therefore when most was required of imagination....Limitations seem always to have been our best friends."

If nothing else, help us to feel positive for having an idea rather than making us feel put down for not thinking of every ramification. Work with us, develop us, so we can learn to think of limitations as spurs to imagination. Set a positive example that says, "Let's make this work!" You'll get much farther with a positive approach that shows your appreciation for our ideas and stresses the useful parts of them.

Besides, imagine how much more fun we would all have—you included—if we came to jobs that were built on the foundation of positivism.

Dear Boss:

Re: **Epilogue**

We all want the same things from our jobs. We want them to be secure and fun. It's that simple.

Feelings of security come from open, honest communications. Tell us the truth, not the party line. Level with us. Be candid, even brutally honest; then we'll know where we stand. When you try to soften the news, you distort it. Trust us with the truth and we'll trust you with our loyalty. And with that basis of trust and loyalty, we'll be even more dedicated and hardworking. You'll look good to your bosses and, therefore, will have greater job security, too.

Without job security we can have little fun because we always harbor that latent fear, "If we lost this job, then what?" Security is only the bedrock upon which to build solid relationships. And yet, job security alone is insufficient. Our work relationships must also be fun.

We know that *fun* is a strange word to use in connection with our jobs. Most people think of their jobs not as fun, but as *work*. But you know and we know that people are more productive when they enjoy what they're doing. Have you ever become involved, really involved, in something that was fun? At some point you probably looked at your watch and noted the time. Then, what seemed like fifteen minutes later, you glanced at your watch again and were startled to find that hours, not minutes, had passed. What happened? You were so involved in doing something enjoyable that the time just rushed past unnoticed. Why can't work be like that, too? Why can't it be fun?

Make our work more fun. Help us plan our careers. Use job rotation, enlargement, and enrichment. Give us more feedback when we do a *good* job. Seek our ideas and use them. Give us recognition for our efforts and ideas. Experiment.

Tom Peters, author of *In Search of Excellence*, wrote, "I believe being out of touch with one's people, vendors and customers, is America's No. 1 managerial problem."[15] Most important is being in touch with your own people. Bosses who are in touch with their own people know whether their people, in turn, are in touch with the vendors and customers. Yet, you're like most bosses we've seen: you remain primarily concerned with how we view you rather than how we feel. So you remain aloof. Come out of your office! Talk with us. Ask us how we can lower costs and improve productivity. We have answers. Want proof? Imagine that the finance department gave you a small briefcase filled with $100 bills. Imagine further that you asked us to report to your office one at a time. And as each of us came in, you slapped a $100 bill down on the desk and said, "It's yours if you can give me one good, usable idea."

Do you think you'd have any $100 bills left? Not likely! Well, if you think you could give away all the $100 bills, then you must believe that we have untapped ideas. Admittedly, not all of our ideas would be useful. But if you sincerely seek and use them, you'll find many money-saving ideas lurking in our minds.

The very act of soliciting our ideas would show you really want them. It would show you really care about costs and productivity. Sending out the traditional memo reminding us of the importance of lower costs, reduced scrap, or higher quality might tell us of your concerns. But actions do speak louder than words! Giving your personal attention even to a few of us would demonstrate that you really care. And if you take our good ideas and use them, we'll know that your commitment is sincere.

So get out of your office! Talk to us. Listen. And use our ideas. Thomas H. Melohn, president and chief executive officer of North American Tool and Die, writes, "Remember, your employees do care. They care very deeply about themselves, their families, their professional progress, and their daily working lives. If you can tap this wellspring and mesh it with the goals of your corporation, the results will truly, absolutely stun you."[16]

Notes

1. Martin S. Davis, "Two Plus Two Doesn't Equal Five," *Fortune* (December 9, 1985): 179.

2. Peter Nulty, "ARCO Is No Sitting Duck," *Fortune* (December 9, 1985): 86.

3. Todd Mason with Marc Frons, "Sam Walton of Wal-Mart: Just Your Basic Homespun Billionaire," *Business Week* (October 14, 1985): 142.

4. William C. Schutz, *Here Comes Everybody* (New York: Harrow Books, 1971), 190.

5. Schutz, *Here Comes Everybody*, 44.

6. It's interesting to note the inherent paradox here: only self-confident bosses are comfortable enough to invite employee input. These bosses know they can do their jobs, so they don't need to prove it to their employees. As a result they're confident enough to risk employee involvements.

7. Walter Kiechel III, "When a Manager Stumbles," *Fortune* (November 12, 1984): 265.

8. Carl C. Icahn, "Now Hear This," *Fortune* (December 9, 1985): 11.

9. M. Scott Peck, *The Road Less Traveled* (New York: Simon & Schuster, 1978), 16.

10. Stewart Troy and Marc Frons, "Mike Dingman Does Deals—and Deals and Deals," *Business Week* (June 17, 1985): 156.

11. "The John Huston Interview," *Playboy* (September 1985): 68.

12. Roger B. Smith, *Commitment-Plus Newsletter* (October, 1985): 2.

13. John F. Akers, "The Spirit of Independence, Part 3: Connections," *INC* (July 1985): 64.

14. Kenneth Blanchard and Spencer Johnson, *The One Minute Manager* (New York: William Morrow and Co., 1982), 39.

15. Tom Peters, "Managers Holed Up in the Office Slip Out of the Mainstream," *Arizona Republic* (May 5, 1985): F9.

16. Thomas H. Melohn, *Commitment-Plus Newletter* (October 1985): 2.

I am now beginning work on a second book of advice for managers. If you have an issue that you would like me to discuss in my next book, or if you have an actual memo you've sent to your boss, I'd love to hear from you. Please write to me at this address:

William B. Werther, Jr.
414 Jenkins Building
Department of Management
School of Business Administration
University of Miami
Coral Gables, Florida 33124